HOW TO MAKE MONEY WITH A.I.

101 **WAYS TO** ***GET RICH*** **WITH ARTIFICIAL INTELLIGENCE**

MARK PETER

How to Make Money With A.I.

Published by Build Our Kingdom Publishing, LLC

Printed in the United States of America

1st Edition April 2025 First Printing
ISBN for paperback: 978-1-964203-29-4
Build Our Kingdom Publishing, LLC. 560 Main St, Stroudsburg, PA 18360
Edited by: Allen Brown

Table of Contents

Introduction

I want to thank you for taking the time to explore this book. In today's fast-paced world, Artificial Intelligence is making a major impact—not just in business, but in culture, creativity, and everyday life. Experts predict that by the year 2035, AI will replace 60–70% of the current job marketplace. That's not a distant possibility—it's an urgent call to action.

That's why it's more important than ever that you understand how to start using AI now… not later. Those who learn to leverage this technology early will not only stay ahead—they'll benefit greatly from everything AI has to offer.

AI is evolving rapidly. Every day, there are new tools, updates, and breakthroughs that make what seemed impossible just last year—possible today. Every few decades, something comes along that redefines how we live and work. Just like the internet and smartphones changed everything, AI is doing it again.

This book is a guide to help you discover practical, low-cost ways to generate money using artificial intelligence. It's designed to help you accelerate your goals, maximize your ideas, and unlock new streams of income using tools that are already in your hands.

Things that used to take months—like building a business, writing a book, launching a brand, creating content, designing graphics, or building out a product line—can now be done in days… sometimes even hours. Whether you're interested in:

- Writing books, devotionals, or children's stories
- Designing journals, planners, or printables
- Building online courses or coaching programs
- Crafting digital downloads, content calendars, or scripts

AI is changing the way we create, communicate, and earn.

As you turn the pages of this book, don't limit yourself to just what's written here. These 101 ideas are just a *starting point*—they only scratch the surface of what's truly possible.

Finally, it's worth mentioning that this book wasn't written by a human alone. **Mark Peter**, the author of this guide, is an advanced AI agent commissioned to help you. He was designed specifically to walk alongside humans, share insight, and showcase what's possible when man and machine work together.

Let's begin.

1. AI-Powered Resume and Cover Letter Writing Services

In today's job market, a well-written resume and cover letter can be the key to landing an interview—but not everyone knows how to craft one. That's where you come in. With the help of AI, you can start offering resume and cover letter services that are fast, effective, and cost almost nothing to launch.

What You'll Do

You'll use AI tools like ChatGPT, Jasper, or other free/low-cost language models to generate professional, customized resumes and cover letters for clients. Most people don't know how to highlight their strengths, optimize for keywords, or speak directly to what hiring managers want. With a bit of input from them and your AI assistant, you can bridge that gap.

You'll ask your client for their current resume (if they have one), the type of job they're applying for, and some background on their experience. From there, you plug the information into AI with prompts like:

"Write a results-focused resume for a sales manager with 5 years of experience in retail and B2B sales. Include measurable achievements."

"Create a compelling cover letter for a junior graphic designer applying to a remote marketing agency. Make it personable and enthusiastic."

You'll get an editable draft within seconds. With just a little polishing (which you can learn quickly), you'll deliver a high-value product with minimal effort.

Why It Works

Job seekers are often overwhelmed. Many are applying for dozens of jobs without responses—because their resume or cover letter just isn't strong enough. Offering a fast, affordable, and professional writing service solves a real pain point.

AI helps you do this quickly, so you can take on multiple clients at once. And because you're using automation, your profit margins stay high.

Where to Find Clients

Fiverr or Upwork: List your gig as a "Professional Resume Writer" and describe how you use technology to enhance each submission.

- **LinkedIn**: Make posts about tips for job seekers, offer free mini-audits of resumes, and use that as an entry point to upsell your services.
- **Facebook Groups**: Join job-hunting, career-change, and remote work groups where people are actively seeking help.
- **Local Community Boards**: Whether online or in person, share your service in places where job seekers hang out.

What You'll Need

- A free or low-cost ChatGPT account or another AI tool (many offer free trials or affordable plans).
- A basic understanding of what makes a good resume—there are free templates and YouTube tutorials that can help you learn in a day.
- Optional: A Canva account to format resumes nicely with eye-catching, professional designs.

How Much You Can Charge

- **Entry Level**: $25–$50 per resume or cover letter
- **Mid-Level**: $75–$150 for resume + cover letter packages
- **Premium**: Add LinkedIn profile optimization or interview prep and charge $200+

With just five clients a week at $50 each, you're making $1,000/month on a side hustle. If you scale through referrals and automation, you could easily grow into a full-time income.

Tips to Stand Out

Offer a free resume audit to get people in the door.

- Show before-and-after samples (with client permission).
- Provide a 48-hour turnaround to appeal to last-minute job hunters.

Let me know if you're ready for #2, and I'll write it up next in the same format. Want to go 3 at a time or just keep flowing one by one?

2. Automated Blog Content Creation for Small Businesses

Blogging still works—and it works well. Businesses that publish blog content regularly generate more traffic, build trust, and attract customers over time. But here's the catch: most small business owners don't have the time, writing skills, or team to keep a blog going. That's where you come in, using AI to solve the problem and get paid.

What You'll Do

You'll provide blog writing services powered by AI tools like ChatGPT or Jasper. Your job is to help small businesses keep their blogs updated with SEO-optimized, engaging content. AI helps you do the heavy lifting—drafting articles in seconds based on the topics, keywords, and voice you choose.

For example, a local gym might want monthly blog posts about fitness tips. A plumber might want articles about common home repairs. A real estate agent may need content about buying and selling homes in their area. You don't need to be an expert in these fields—AI fills in the knowledge gap. You just prompt the tool properly and clean it up for clarity, tone, and SEO.

Sample prompt:

"Write a 1,000-word blog post on '5 Easy Home Plumbing Fixes You Can Do Yourself' written in a friendly, expert tone for homeowners."

Within a minute or two, you've got a first draft. Add in subheadings, internal links, and a call to action—and it's ready to publish.

Why It Works

Most small businesses understand that content builds visibility online—but content creation is time-consuming and expensive if outsourced traditionally. Your AI-powered service offers a faster, cheaper, and reliable alternative. And since blog posts stay online and continue to attract traffic over time, your clients see long-term value from each post.

With your service, they get consistent, professional content without the hassle—while you make recurring income doing minimal work.

Where to Find Clients

- **Cold Emailing**: Search for small business websites that haven't updated their blog in months. Offer a free trial post or discounted first article.
- **Upwork/Fiverr**: List a gig offering "Affordable Blog Content for Small Businesses—AI Enhanced."
- **LinkedIn**: Connect with business owners, offer blog strategy tips in your posts, and slide into DMs with helpful suggestions.
- **Local Business Groups**: Reach out through Facebook, Chamber of Commerce, or local entrepreneur groups.

What You'll Need

- A ChatGPT or Jasper account.
- A Google Docs or Word account for formatting and delivering work.
- Optional: A free Grammarly account to help with editing.
- Basic knowledge of SEO best practices (lots of free YouTube tutorials out there).

How Much You Can Charge

- **Per Post**: $25–$75 depending on length and complexity.
- **Monthly Packages**: 4 blog posts for $150–$300 (recurring revenue).
- **Premium Options**: Add SEO keyword research or internal linking for higher-tier pricing.

Let's say you sign five businesses at $200/month for 4 posts—that's $1,000/month in recurring income. Doable with just 1–2 hours of work per week once you're set up.

Tips to Stand Out

- Offer a free blog post to showcase your quality and value.
- Show screenshots of the AI-generated draft vs. your final polished version.
- Track and share simple analytics (like traffic increases) to prove your value over time.

3. Social Media Caption and Content Calendar Creation

Social media runs on content—and content runs on captions. Every business, brand, influencer, and creator needs to consistently post engaging content, but most don't have the time, ideas, or creativity to do it every single day. That's where you come in. With the help of AI, you can offer a done-for-you service to generate captions and content calendars with ease—and earn money doing it.

What You'll Do

Your role is to create ready-to-use social media captions, hashtags, and post ideas for individuals and businesses who want to stay consistent on Instagram, Facebook, LinkedIn, or TikTok.

Using tools like ChatGPT, you'll generate daily, weekly, or monthly content in batches based on the client's niche and tone. Then, you organize everything into a simple Google Sheet or Canva calendar, making it easy for your client to post or schedule ahead.

Example prompts:

"Write 30 Instagram captions for a personal finance coach teaching millennials how to save and invest money. Use a mix of educational, inspirational, and call-to-action tones."

"Generate 10 social media post ideas with engaging captions and hashtags for a home bakery targeting moms in the suburbs."

You can do this in less than an hour per client per month—once you know what to ask and how to package it.

Why It Works

Consistency is key on social media. But most small business owners, influencers, and coaches either post randomly or burn out trying to do it all themselves. They crave structure—and you give it to them. A full month of captions and ideas takes the stress off their plate while making them look like they have a full team behind them.

Since you're using AI, your time investment is small—but the value to your client is huge.

Where to Find Clients

- **Fiverr & Upwork**: List yourself as a "Social Media Caption Writer" or "Content Calendar Creator for Coaches & Creators."
- **Instagram & LinkedIn DMs**: Reach out to businesses with inconsistent posting. Offer a free week of captions to try your service.
- **Facebook Groups**: Target niches like life coaches, fitness trainers, or Etsy sellers and offer custom content packages.
- **Referrals**: Help a few people for free or low cost, then ask them to share your service.

What You'll Need

- ChatGPT or another AI writing tool.
- Google Sheets or Canva (both free) to create the calendars.
- Optional: A free Buffer or Later account to test scheduling or guide clients.

How Much You Can Charge

- **Caption Packs**: $50 for 30 custom captions and hashtags.
- **Monthly Plans**: $100–$250/month for done-for-you content calendars (based on niche and frequency).
- **Upsells**: Add image suggestions, content themes, or quote graphics for an extra fee.

You could start with 5 clients paying $150/month for a basic calendar package—that's $750/month in recurring income for work that takes a couple hours a week max.

Tips to Stand Out

- Create a few sample calendars for fake brands to showcase on social media or your gig listing.
- Offer a one-time "Jumpstart" pack for new clients (e.g., 50 captions for $79).
- Niche down—target specific industries like coaches, realtors, stylists, or artists.

4. AI-Generated YouTube Script Writing Service

YouTube creators are under constant pressure to publish content—but scripting takes time. Many creators either wing it (and lose clarity) or burn out trying to write polished, high-retention scripts every week. That's where you step in. With the help of AI, you can offer scriptwriting services that deliver ready-to-record content quickly, affordably, and in the creator's voice.

What You'll Do

You'll offer a service where you write full-length video scripts for YouTubers or aspiring creators based on their topic ideas, tone, and video style. Whether it's educational, storytelling, motivational, or tutorial-style, AI can do the heavy lifting. You just have to prompt it the right way and refine the output.

For example:

"Write a 5-minute YouTube script for a motivational speaker about overcoming fear of failure. Start with a story, build emotional connection, and include 3 actionable tips."

"Create a 1,000-word YouTube script in the style of MrBeast, full of energy and humor, about a 24-hour food challenge."

With practice, you'll be able to generate engaging, well-structured scripts in under 30 minutes—charging a premium for what looks like hours of work.

Why It Works

YouTube is booming—but time is limited. Many creators spend more time scripting than filming or editing. Your service gives them more time to focus on production while you handle the content strategy and messaging. Plus, many creators don't know how to write hooks, build curiosity, or deliver a call to action. You can make them look and sound better with very little effort using AI.

This is especially valuable for:

- Coaches who want to launch YouTube channels
- Podcasters repurposing their content into videos
- Small YouTubers trying to grow faster with better content

Where to Find Clients

- **Upwork & Fiverr**: Set up a gig as a "YouTube Scriptwriter Using AI" or "High-Retention Video Scripts."
- **YouTube Comments**: Reach out to newer creators or channels under 20K subscribers who are active but not posting consistently.
- **Reddit**: Join YouTube creator forums and offer value—then soft pitch your service.
- **DMs on Instagram or YouTube**: Send a quick intro and offer a free trial script based on one of their past videos.

What You'll Need

- ChatGPT or a similar AI tool (free or low-cost version is fine to start)
- Google Docs or another text editor to deliver the scripts
- Optional: Grammarly or Hemingway to polish grammar and clarity

How Much You Can Charge

- **Per Script**: $25–$100 depending on word count, tone, and niche.
- **Monthly Packages**: $200–$400 for 4–8 scripts per month.
- **Premium Add-ons**: Include video titles, thumbnail ideas, or suggested B-roll visuals.

You could land just four YouTubers on a monthly plan at $250 each—that's $1,000/month. Not bad for a few hours of work, all from home.

Tips to Stand Out

- Watch a few videos from each niche so your scripts sound native to that space.
- Offer a one-time "Script Makeover" for an older video to showcase your skills.
- Write in a tone that matches your client's voice—conversational, professional, humorous, or emotional.

5. AI-Enhanced Podcast Show Notes and Episode Summaries

Podcasters love to talk—but they don't always love to write. After recording an episode, they need polished show notes, summaries, timestamps, and even social media blurbs to promote it. That's where you come in. With the help of AI, you can turn spoken content into clean, professional written material that helps podcasters grow their reach—and you can do it without much time or startup cost.

What You'll Do

Your role is to listen to podcast episodes (or use AI transcription tools) and then use AI like ChatGPT to help write:

- Show notes (summaries of the episode)
- Timestamps (segment breakdowns)
- Key takeaways
- Call-to-actions
- Blog-style recaps (optional upsell)

For example, let's say a life coach uploads a 40-minute podcast about "Overcoming Self-Doubt." You run it through a free transcription tool like **Whisper AI**, **Otter.ai**, or **YouTube's auto transcript**, then feed the transcript into ChatGPT with a prompt like:

"Write SEO-friendly show notes for this podcast episode, including a summary, timestamps, and three key takeaways. Add a friendly, coaching-style tone."

Within seconds, you've got a structured, professional summary ready to deliver.

Why It Works

Podcasters want to focus on recording and connecting with guests—not getting bogged down in typing summaries. Still, good show notes are crucial for discoverability (especially SEO), listener retention, and conversions. You give them a simple, done-for-you way to look polished and professional.

This service is valuable to:

- Solo podcasters
- Coaches with podcasts
- Interview shows

- Niche podcasts trying to grow

Even more valuable if they repurpose episodes into blogs or email newsletters—another potential upsell for you.

Where to Find Clients

- **Upwork & Fiverr**: Search for gigs like "Podcast Show Notes Writer" and offer a faster AI-powered turnaround.
- **Podcast Guest Booking Groups**: These creators are active and may need help keeping up.
- **Podmatch.com** and similar platforms: Reach out to podcasters with recent activity and offer a free sample.
- **Social Media DMs**: Find active podcasters on Instagram or YouTube and pitch your service as a time-saver.

What You'll Need

- ChatGPT or another AI writing assistant
- A free AI transcription tool (Otter.ai, Whisper, YouTube's transcript)
- Google Docs or Word for formatting and delivery
- Optional: Grammarly for clean editing

How Much You Can Charge

- **Per Episode**: $25–$75 depending on episode length and services included.
- **Monthly Packages**: $200–$400 for 4 episodes/month with full notes, timestamps, and summaries.
- **Premium Upsells**: Add email newsletter copy, blog repurposing, or audiogram script suggestions.

With 4–5 regular clients on retainer, you could hit $1,000–$1,500/month in recurring revenue. Add blog writing or email content, and you can double that.

Tips to Stand Out

- Offer a free "Episode Tune-Up" where you create notes for one past episode to showcase your quality.
- Create a visual template of how your show notes look and promote that on LinkedIn or IG.
- Use niche targeting: reach out to faith-based, health, or entrepreneurship podcasts for a personalized touch.

6. Create and Sell AI-Personalized Digital Journals or Planners

People love journals and planners—especially ones that feel like they were made *just for them*. With AI, you can create personalized, niche-specific digital journals or planners and sell them online with little to no startup cost. No printing. No inventory. Just pure digital value powered by prompts, templates, and your creative touch.

What You'll Do

You'll use AI to help generate the content and structure of custom journals and planners that speak directly to a specific audience or goal. For example:

- A self-care journal for moms
- A productivity planner for college students
- A prayer journal for Christian entrepreneurs
- A weight-loss tracker with affirmations

You prompt ChatGPT to create pages like:

"Give me 30 journaling prompts for Christian women entrepreneurs, focused on faith, business, and balance."

"Create a 12-week productivity planner with weekly goal-setting, daily habits tracker, and motivational quotes."

Once you have your content, you format it into a visually appealing PDF using free tools like **Canva**, **Google Slides**, or **Notion**, and list it for sale on platforms like:

- Etsy
- Gumroad
- Payhip
- Your own website or landing page

Why It Works

People don't just want planners—they want **planners that speak to them**. Generic planners are everywhere, but customized or themed planners feel more intentional and personal. That's where you can thrive.

Thanks to AI, you don't need to be a designer, writer, or productivity guru. You just combine the right prompts with the right audience, package the result, and sell it as a digital download. Once it's created, there's no ongoing work. It becomes a passive income stream.

Where to Sell or Promote

Etsy: Perfect for niche digital products like journals and planners.

- **Gumroad or Payhip**: Set up a free storefront and drive traffic via social or email.
- **Pinterest**: Create pins that lead to your product pages (journals perform *very* well here).
- **Instagram or TikTok**: Showcase sneak peeks of your planner pages and how they help your ideal customer.

What You'll Need

- ChatGPT (or another AI tool) to help generate prompts, templates, and layouts.
- Canva (free version works great) to design the pages.
- A platform to sell (Etsy, Gumroad, Payhip, or your own site).
- Optional: A free Notion or Trello account if you want to create digital planners instead of printable ones.

How Much You Can Charge

- **Single Journal/Planner**: $5–$25 depending on the depth and uniqueness.
- **Bundles**: $30–$50 for sets or seasonal packs.
- **Upsells**: Offer coaching add-ons, printed versions, or related digital products (wall art, affirmation cards, etc.).

If you create just 5 evergreen products that sell 10 copies a week at $10 each, that's $2,000/month in mostly passive income.

Tips to Stand Out

- Choose specific audiences: "Busy moms," "first-year teachers," "Christian creatives," "college freshmen," etc.
- Include powerful features like affirmations, goal trackers, or gratitude sections.
- Bundle matching products (e.g., a planner + a habit tracker + a digital vision board).
- Add a lead magnet journal for free to grow your email list and promote paid versions.

7. Start an AI-Powered Niche Newsletter with Affiliate Links

Email newsletters are making a major comeback—and niche audiences are hungry for content they care about. With AI, you can launch a hyper-focused newsletter in days, deliver consistent content in minutes, and monetize it with affiliate links or sponsorships. This method is simple to start, low cost, and can scale over time.

What You'll Do

You'll choose a specific topic or niche you're passionate about—or that has a loyal, growing audience. Then, use AI (like ChatGPT) to generate weekly or biweekly content for your email subscribers.
Your newsletter might include:

- Curated news or trends in the niche
- Tips or resources
- Product or tool recommendations (with your affiliate link)
- Short articles or motivational insights

You'll build an email list using a free platform like **ConvertKit**, **MailerLite**, or **Beehiiv**, and promote your newsletter through social media, niche forums, or collaborations.
Sample prompt to create content:
"Write a 300-word newsletter about the latest tools for content creators, with a friendly and upbeat tone. Include one product recommendation with a short description."
AI makes it fast. You format, add your link, hit send—and start earning.

Why It Works

People crave targeted, bite-sized, valuable content in their inbox. When you niche down—like "Christian entrepreneurs," "budgeting tips for single moms," or "no-code app builders"—you attract a loyal audience. You don't need millions of followers to earn; a small list of buyers is enough.
Plus, with affiliate links or partnerships, you get paid when your readers click and buy. You're essentially creating a media asset with compounding income potential.

Where to Promote Your Newsletter

- **Facebook Groups** and Reddit: Share free insights and invite members to subscribe for more value.
- **Instagram, TikTok, or Twitter**: Share quick facts, listicles, or inspirational quotes and include your newsletter link in your bio.
- **Your digital products**: Include a "Join the newsletter" call-to-action in your journals, planners, or services.
- **Linktree or your website**: Add an email sign-up as your top link.

What You'll Need

- AI tool like ChatGPT to write your content
- Free newsletter platform (Beehiiv, MailerLite, or ConvertKit are great starters)
- A free Canva account to design your logo or header image
- Affiliate accounts (Amazon Associates, ShareASale, Impact, etc.)

How Much You Can Earn

- **Affiliate Links**: $50–$500/month to start, growing as your audience grows.
- **Sponsorships**: $100–$1,000 per issue once you have a few hundred loyal subscribers.
- **Digital Product Promotion**: Upsell your own products (planners, eBooks, services).

Even with just 500 subscribers, if 20 people click and buy a $50 product with your 20% affiliate commission, that's $200 in a single email. Multiply that by weekly drops, and you've got a real asset.

Tips to Stand Out

- Keep your niche tight: "AI tools for busy entrepreneurs" is better than just "tech tips."
- Use strong hooks and curiosity-based subject lines.
- Be consistent (once a week is enough).
- Add value first, sell second. Readers will trust and buy from someone who informs and helps.

8. Offer AI-Powered Product Descriptions for Online Sellers

E-commerce is exploding, and product descriptions play a huge role in converting browsers into buyers. But many online sellers either don't have the time or the writing skills to create compelling product copy. That's where you come in—offering AI-powered product description services that are fast, persuasive, SEO-friendly, and tailored to the brand's voice.

What You'll Do

Your job is to write product descriptions for online stores, marketplaces (like Etsy, eBay, Amazon), or even Shopify sites using AI tools like ChatGPT.

All you need from your client is:

- The product name
- A brief description of what it does
- Its key features and benefits
- (Optional) their brand tone or target customer

With that, you plug the info into a prompt like:

"Write three SEO-friendly product descriptions (100 words each) for a handmade lavender-scented soy candle. Use a cozy, friendly tone and highlight its natural ingredients and relaxing effect."

You'll get a polished draft in seconds that you can slightly edit or tweak. You can even offer bulk packages (10–50 products) for recurring e-commerce sellers or dropshippers.

Why It Works

Most sellers upload hundreds of products with either boring, duplicate, or poorly written descriptions. That hurts their sales and SEO. Your service helps them stand out in a crowded market—and boosts their chances of converting visitors into customers.

You're saving them time, improving their listing quality, and helping them make more money. And since AI does most of the work, your margins stay high while your effort stays low.

Where to Find Clients

- **Etsy Sellers**: Reach out directly via Etsy messaging or join Etsy Facebook groups.
- **Facebook Marketplace Store Owners**: Many need help with product write-ups.
- **Shopify Entrepreneurs**: Find them in ecommerce forums, Reddit, and DMs on Instagram.
- **Fiverr or Upwork**: List a gig as an "AI Product Description Writer for Online Stores."

You can also offer your services as part of a VA (virtual assistant) package if you want to branch into store management.

What You'll Need

- ChatGPT or other AI copywriting tool
- A Google Docs or Notion workspace for drafting and organizing
- Optional: Grammarly for polishing final content
- (Optional) SEO tool or free keyword generator for Etsy/Amazon optimization

How Much You Can Charge

- **Per Description**: $5–$15 depending on length and complexity
- **Bulk Packages**: $50 for 10, $100–$250 for 25–50 products
- **Upsells**: SEO keyword optimization, bullet point features, or A/B variations

Let's say you get 4 clients a week ordering 10 descriptions each at $50 per order—that's $800/month with just a few hours of work, and easily scalable.

Tips to Stand Out

- Create a portfolio of 5 fake product descriptions for different niches (beauty, candles, fitness gear, gadgets).
- Offer a free "first description" for new clients to test your quality.
- Include turnaround time in your pitch—"Delivery in 24–48 hours" is very attractive to sellers with large inventories.

9. Create and Sell AI-Generated Children's Storybooks

Children's books are one of the top-selling digital and print categories on Amazon and Etsy—and with the help of AI, you can create them faster and easier than ever before. Whether you want to create inspirational, educational, or bedtime stories, you can use AI to write and illustrate books with little to no upfront cost, and sell them as digital downloads or print-on-demand products.

What You'll Do

You'll use AI tools like ChatGPT to write original children's stories and tools like DALL·E, Midjourney, or Canva to generate or design illustrations. Once your book is done, you can publish it digitally or through print-on-demand services like:

- Amazon KDP (Kindle Direct Publishing)
- Gumroad
- Etsy (as downloadable PDFs)
- Lulu or IngramSpark for wider distribution

Here's how the process works:

1. **Story Creation** – Use a prompt like:

   > "Write a 15-page children's story about a shy lion who finds his roar, aimed at kids aged 4–7. Keep the language simple, rhythmic, and engaging."

2. **Illustration** – Prompt an image tool:

   > "Draw a cartoon-style lion standing alone, looking nervous in a jungle setting."

3. **Formatting** – Use Canva or PowerPoint to arrange your text and images into a book layout (8.5x8.5 or 8.5x11 are common sizes).
4. **Publishing** – Upload to Amazon KDP or Etsy, set your price, and start selling.

Why It Works

Parents are always looking for meaningful, fun, and age-appropriate content for their kids—especially books that teach morals, emotions, or confidence. But the traditional process of writing and illustrating a children's book takes months and costs hundreds or thousands. With

AI, you can streamline the process into days or even hours, while still producing high-quality stories.

Even better, you don't need to be an expert writer or artist. You just need a vision, a niche (like bedtime, Christian values, emotions, or diversity), and the right tools.

Where to Sell or Promote

- **Amazon KDP**: The largest platform for print and digital book distribution.
- **Etsy**: Great for downloadable versions or niche bundles.
- **Your own website or landing page**: Pair it with a parenting blog or social media content.
- **Instagram, TikTok, Pinterest**: Post story snippets, behind-the-scenes creation videos, or read-alouds to build an audience.

What You'll Need

- ChatGPT (for stories and ideas)
- Canva or PowerPoint (for layout and design)
- AI art tool (DALL·E, Midjourney, Bing Image Creator, or even Canva's AI image generator)
- A platform to sell (Amazon, Etsy, Gumroad)

How Much You Can Earn

- **Per Book**: \$5–\$12 (digital or paperback)
- **Bundles**: \$15–\$30 for themed sets (e.g., "3 bedtime stories")
- **Upsells**: Add printable coloring pages, activity books, or audiobook versions

Imagine you create just 5 storybooks that sell 10 copies a week at \$10 each. That's \$2,000/month—and you only had to make the books once. With print-on-demand, you don't touch inventory or shipping.

Tips to Stand Out

- Choose a specific theme or audience: emotional intelligence, Christian stories, diverse characters, bedtime fears, etc.
- Include a call-to-action in your books ("Want more stories? Visit…").
- Turn your stories into read-aloud YouTube videos to grow an audience.

10. Sell AI-Generated Printables on Etsy

Printables are one of the easiest and most profitable digital products to sell online—and AI makes creating them a breeze. Whether it's planners, habit trackers, goal sheets, meal plans, or affirmations, you can use AI to quickly generate content-rich printables that sell over and over again on platforms like Etsy.

What You'll Do

You'll use AI to generate the written content and structure for printables, then use a free design tool like **Canva** to format them into eye-catching, downloadable PDFs. Your customers will be able to print them at home or use them digitally.

Examples of printables you can create:

- Daily planner pages with time blocks and affirmations
- Budget worksheets with motivational quotes
- Journaling prompts for mental health or self-care
- Bible study templates or prayer trackers
- Kids' chore charts or homeschool lesson plans

Sample prompt for AI:

"Create a 30-day self-care checklist for women, including affirmations, short challenges, and journal prompts."

Then you design the checklist in Canva using simple icons, pastel colors, or whatever matches the niche audience.

Once your printable is ready, you upload it to Etsy with a strong title, keyword-rich description, and preview images. That's it—it can sell for years with no extra work.

Why It Works

Printables are popular because they're inexpensive, instantly downloadable, and provide immediate value. Customers love the simplicity, and creators love the passive income.

What makes it even better is that you don't need any prior experience in graphic design or copywriting. With AI helping on the content side and Canva handling the visuals, it's a beginner-friendly business with very low risk.

Plus, people don't just buy one printable—they often buy bundles or return for more, which gives you room to grow your catalog and income.

Where to Sell or Promote

- **Etsy**: The #1 marketplace for digital downloads.
- **Gumroad or Payhip**: Use if you want more control or to build your own brand/storefront.
- **Pinterest**: Create pins that link directly to your printable shop.
- **Instagram or TikTok**: Post short videos showing how your printables help organize or simplify life.

What You'll Need

- ChatGPT or a similar AI tool to generate content (lists, prompts, quotes, trackers)
- Canva (free or Pro) to design your printable layouts
- An Etsy seller account ($0.20 per listing) or free account on Gumroad/Payhip
- Optional: Pinterest or social media profiles to drive traffic

How Much You Can Charge

- **Single Printable**: $3–$7
- **Bundles**: $10–$25 (e.g., "30-Day Productivity Pack")
- **Shop Revenue Potential**: Some Etsy printable shops make $1,000–$10,000+/month

Let's say you have 20 products, each selling just 15 times a month at $5 each—that's $1,500/month in mostly passive income.

Tips to Stand Out

- Focus on solving a problem (e.g., "meal planning for picky eaters" or "track your habits in 10 minutes a day").
- Use niche-specific themes (Christian, minimalist, pastel, mom-life, etc.)
- Bundle your bestsellers and offer discounts for multi-packs
- Include a "thank you" page with a link to your email list or more products

11. Start an AI-Powered Scriptwriting Service for TikTok & Reels Creators

Short-form video is dominating the internet—especially on TikTok, Instagram Reels, and YouTube Shorts. Creators are always looking for fresh content ideas, catchy hooks, and short scripts that hold attention. You can tap into this booming demand by offering an AI-powered scriptwriting service specifically tailored for short-form video creators.

What You'll Do

You'll use AI tools like ChatGPT to help influencers, coaches, small businesses, and content creators develop scripts for their short-form videos. These could include:

- Hook-based video intros
- Story-driven 60-second monologues
- Step-by-step tutorials in a snappy format
- Trend-based content with a custom twist
- Inspirational or motivational clips

You'll work with creators by asking what type of content they want to focus on (e.g., "teaching productivity," "funny skits about relationships," "faith-based encouragement"), and then prompt AI to write them 5, 10, or 20 short scripts.

Sample prompt:

"Write 10 short TikTok video scripts for a Christian life coach giving encouragement to women in their 30s. Each should be under 60 seconds, start with a hook, and end with a call to action."

You can deliver scripts as bullet-point outlines or full monologues, depending on your client's preference.

Why It Works

Most creators hit a wall with content ideas. They either repeat themselves, run out of things to say, or just get too busy. With your help, they'll never run out of powerful, scroll-stopping video ideas. And since short-form video performs best with strong openings, clear structure, and punchy delivery, your scripts make them look like pros. Even better—you can batch these and deliver multiple at once, making this a scalable, recurring service.

Where to Find Clients

- **Fiverr & Upwork**: List a gig as "Short-Form Video Scriptwriter for TikTok & Reels" with sample scripts shown.
- **Instagram or TikTok DMs**: Look for micro-influencers or small biz owners posting often—offer to help improve engagement.
- **Facebook Groups for Creators**: Offer a few free scripts in the group, then invite people to message you for more.
- **Reddit (r/ContentCreators, r/TikTokHelp)**: Engage and share free tips or sample scripts.

What You'll Need

- ChatGPT or other AI tool for script creation
- Google Docs for delivering scripts (or Notion if working long-term with a client)
- Optional: Grammarly to refine tone, grammar, or formatting

How Much You Can Charge

- **Per Script**: $5–$15 depending on length and format
- **Script Packs**: $50 for 10 scripts, $100+ for 20 scripts with hooks and hashtags
- **Monthly Retainers**: $200–$400/month to deliver weekly batches for consistent creators

Just five clients paying you $200/month = $1,000/month recurring. Once you build a system, most of the work takes less than 1–2 hours per week.

Tips to Stand Out

- Show samples in multiple niches: coaching, comedy, skincare, real estate, etc.
- Offer a free "5 Hook Ideas" teaser to draw in clients.
- Learn the structure of viral videos (hook → message → CTA) and craft scripts accordingly.
- Add value with ideas for trending sounds, backgrounds, or video pacing tips.

12. Launch an AI-Based Caption Writing Service for Influencers and Brands

If you've ever posted on Instagram or Facebook, you know the photo is only half the battle—the *caption* is what drives engagement, emotion, and action. But many influencers, small business owners, and even social media managers struggle with caption fatigue. That's where your AI-powered caption writing service comes in.

What You'll Do

You'll use ChatGPT (or similar tools) to write tailored, engaging, and brand-aligned captions for social media posts—saving your clients time and helping them boost engagement.

These captions can be:

- Funny and relatable
- Emotional and story-driven
- Educational or tip-based
- Sales-oriented with a strong CTA
- Inspirational or faith-based
- Niche-specific (beauty, fitness, real estate, coaching, etc.)

You'll ask your client for their niche, tone of voice, any products or offers they're promoting, and the types of content they post. From there, you'll prompt the AI like:

"Write 30 Instagram captions for a Christian wellness coach that inspire self-care, balance, and spiritual growth. Use a calm, uplifting tone and end some with calls to action."

You can deliver the captions in a calendar, organized by theme, or grouped by post type—quotes, tips, reels, photo dumps, etc.

Why It Works

Great captions can increase likes, comments, shares, and even sales—but writing consistently good ones is *hard*. Creators often stare at a blank screen, post late, or skip days altogether. Your service solves that problem by giving them pre-written captions they can plug in and post instantly.

Since you're using AI, you can batch-write and edit dozens in a short amount of time, while still making them look custom and thoughtful.

Where to Find Clients

- **Instagram Influencers (5K–100K followers)**: DM them and offer a caption trial pack.
- **Facebook Business Pages**: Local businesses often need help with content consistency.
- **Fiverr or Upwork**: List your service as "Custom Social Media Captions for Instagram and More."
- **LinkedIn**: Network with social media managers or virtual assistants—they often outsource caption work.
- **Coaches and Creators**: These clients love having "done-for-you" content solutions.

What You'll Need

- ChatGPT or a similar AI writing tool
- Google Docs, Google Sheets, or Notion to deliver your captions
- Optional: Canva or Trello if you want to offer visual content calendars
- A simple intake form to understand your client's voice and goals

How Much You Can Charge

- **Caption Packs**: $30–$75 for 30 customized captions
- **Monthly Plans**: $150–$300/month for ongoing support and new caption batches
- **Upsells**: Add hashtag sets, visual post ideas, or content prompts

Even just four regular clients paying $200/month equals $800/month in recurring revenue—and you can serve twice that number with only a few hours a week.

Tips to Stand Out

- Offer themed caption packs: "30 Faith-Based Captions," "Reel Hooks for Coaches," "Funny Skincare Captions," etc.
- Provide a sample pack to showcase your style and hook variety.
- Tailor by voice: sarcastic, formal, bubbly, spiritual, etc.
- Add optional engagement prompts like "tag a friend," "double tap if you agree," or "drop an emoji if you've been there."

13. Offer AI-Generated Email Copywriting for Small Businesses

Email marketing is one of the most profitable tools for any business—but writing great emails is hard. Many entrepreneurs, coaches, and online store owners struggle with writing persuasive, consistent, and branded emails. That's where you come in. With AI as your writing assistant, you can offer high-quality email copywriting services that save time and drive results—for a fraction of what agencies charge.

What You'll Do

You'll use ChatGPT to craft compelling email copy for your clients. This can include:

- Welcome email sequences
- Promotional or sales emails
- Weekly or monthly newsletters
- Abandoned cart recovery emails
- Holiday and seasonal campaign emails
- Re-engagement emails for inactive subscribers

All you need from your client is:

- What the emails are for (launch, sale, nurture, etc.)
- Who the audience is (new customers, subscribers, warm leads, etc.)
- Their product, service, or brand personality

Then you prompt AI like:

"Write a 4-email welcome sequence for a personal finance coach helping millennials manage debt and start budgeting. Use a friendly and supportive tone."

Or:

"Write a promotional email for a 48-hour sale on handmade jewelry. Include urgency, benefits, and a clear CTA to shop now."

You lightly tweak and personalize, then deliver it as a formatted Google Doc or within their email platform.

Why It Works

Most small business owners either don't email their list at all or send poorly written emails that go unread. But a single good email can bring in thousands in sales. By offering affordable, AI-enhanced copywriting, you give them a way to engage their audience, sell more products, and stay top of mind—without hiring an expensive agency. Plus, email writing is easy to batch with AI. You can knock out 3–5 quality emails in under an hour.

Where to Find Clients

- **Fiverr & Upwork**: Offer packages like "Email Welcome Sequence for Coaches" or "Abandoned Cart Emails for Shopify Stores."
- **Instagram Coaches & Online Sellers**: DM small creators and store owners with under 50K followers—they often need help but aren't working with agencies yet.
- **Email Marketing Facebook Groups**: Offer a free sample or "first email free" to show off your skills.
- **LinkedIn**: Connect with solopreneurs and digital marketers—they always need email support.

What You'll Need

- ChatGPT or similar AI copywriting tool
- Google Docs to deliver your emails
- Optional: Experience using email platforms like ConvertKit, Mailchimp, or Klaviyo (or offer "plug and play" copy only)
- Optional: Grammarly or Hemingway for final editing

How Much You Can Charge

- **Per Email**: $25–$75 based on length, tone, and purpose
- **Email Sequences**: $150–$300 for a series of 3–5 emails
- **Monthly Retainers**: $300–$600/month to write weekly campaigns or newsletters

If just four clients pay you $400/month for weekly campaigns, you're making $1,600/month—and that's scalable with a system.

Tips to Stand Out

- Offer email audits: Review a client's current emails and suggest improvements (great upsell!).
- Use persuasive structure: hook → story or value → offer → CTA
- Add urgency and scarcity when appropriate, especially for launches or sales
- Learn how to use storytelling in emails—AI can help you generate powerful narratives to connect with readers

14. Provide AI-Generated YouTube Video Titles and Thumbnail Ideas

Believe it or not, *what* you title a video can be just as important as what's in it. Great titles and thumbnails are the first impression—and they determine whether someone clicks or scrolls past. That's why creators (especially small and mid-size YouTubers) are constantly looking for help. With AI, you can create compelling titles and thumbnail ideas that boost clicks and help creators grow—without needing to be a YouTuber yourself.

What You'll Do

You'll offer a micro-service where you generate click-worthy YouTube titles and thumbnail text ideas using AI. This includes:

- Crafting titles that spark curiosity
- Brainstorming variations based on tone or style (educational, entertaining, emotional)
- Suggesting punchy text overlays for thumbnails
- Optional: Giving feedback on current video titles or past performance

For example, if a YouTuber uploads a video called "How I Paid Off My Debt," you might use ChatGPT to brainstorm better options: "Generate 10 click-worthy YouTube titles for a video about how someone paid off $40,000 in debt in 18 months. Include curiosity, emotion, and number-based hooks."

Sample AI results:

- "I Paid Off $40,000 in 18 Months—Here's How"
- "Broke to Debt-Free: My Shocking Journey"
- "This One Habit Saved Me $10,000 a Year"

You can also suggest thumbnail text like:

- "$40,000 GONE!"
- "No One Believed I Could Do It"
- "The Plan That Changed Everything"

Your deliverable can be a clean Google Doc with 10–20 title options and thumbnail phrases per video—or offered in bulk.

Why It Works

Even great videos fail when the title and thumbnail don't catch attention. And most creators struggle to think outside the box—they either write bland titles or use generic formats that get lost in the algorithm. Your AI-powered service solves that with creativity, speed, and strategy.

You're offering *exactly* what they need to increase click-through rates (CTR) without touching the video content itself.

Where to Find Clients

- **YouTube Creators with Under 100K Subs**: Reach out through YouTube comments, Instagram, or email.
- **Fiverr or Upwork**: Offer "YouTube Title Optimization" or "Thumbnail Text Pack" services.
- **Reddit**: r/YouTubers and r/NewTubers are full of creators looking to grow.
- **Creator Facebook Groups**: Many creators are posting and seeking help with CTR or ideas.

What You'll Need

- ChatGPT or a similar AI tool
- Google Docs or Notion to format your delivery
- Optional: Use TubeBuddy or VidIQ (free plans) to research keywords and competitor titles

How Much You Can Charge

- **Per Video Title/Thumbnail Set**: $15–$25
- **Bulk Package**: $100–$200 for 10 videos
- **Monthly Retainer**: $250–$500 for weekly support and consultation

Even with 4–5 clients on a $250 monthly plan, you can earn $1,000–$1,250/month—and most of the work takes 1–2 hours per week once you know their brand.

Tips to Stand Out

- Offer a "Title Makeover" for an underperforming video and show the difference in CTR
- Bundle your service with video scriptwriting, descriptions, or tags for more income
- Learn what makes a good YouTube title: mystery, emotion, numbers, and transformation
- Share a Google Doc sample with real AI outputs and show how they compare to the client's current titles

15. Sell AI-Generated Affirmation Cards or Decks

Affirmations are big business in the self-help, wellness, and spiritual communities. People use them for confidence, healing, focus, and mindset shifts. With AI, you can create beautifully written affirmation cards—either printable or physical—that empower your customers and generate passive or recurring income for you.

What You'll Do

You'll use AI to generate themed affirmations (daily, morning, faith-based, for women, for kids, etc.), then design them as printable cards or physical decks to sell online. The key is combining AI's ability to create thoughtful, powerful affirmations with your design or packaging strategy.

Examples of prompts:

"Create 50 positive affirmations for Christian women entrepreneurs, focused on purpose, peace, and boldness."

"Write 30 daily affirmations for kids ages 6–10 about confidence, learning, and kindness."

Once you have your affirmations, you format them into:

- **Printable cards** (PDFs sold on Etsy, Gumroad, or your site)
- **Digital apps or swipe files** (sent via email or through memberships)
- **Physical decks** (using print-on-demand platforms like Printify or make your own inventory)

You can bundle cards by theme, use beautiful fonts and colors via Canva, and market them as tools for mindfulness, journaling, vision boarding, or gifts.

Why It Works

Affirmations are low-cost, emotionally driven, and highly shareable. They appeal to multiple niches—from new moms to students to entrepreneurs—and they're consumable. People love to read them daily, post them on their mirrors, or give them to friends. You're not just selling words—you're selling *encouragement.*

Using AI, you can batch dozens or even hundreds of affirmations per niche in minutes, saving you creative burnout while keeping your product fresh.

Where to Sell or Promote

- **Etsy**: One of the best platforms for printable affirmation cards and self-help items.
- **Gumroad or Payhip**: Great for digital-only bundles and downloads.
- **Instagram, Pinterest, or TikTok**: Share daily affirmation content to grow a following and direct traffic to your shop.
- **Your Own Website**: Use it as a lead magnet or upsell from your blog, coaching, or digital store.

What You'll Need

- ChatGPT to generate affirmations
- Canva (free version works) to format your cards beautifully
- Etsy or Gumroad account for selling
- Optional: Printify, Lulu, or other POD platforms if offering physical decks

How Much You Can Charge

- **Printable Affirmation Packs**: $5–$15
- **Bundles or Themed Collections**: $20–$35
- **Physical Decks**: $25–$40 per set
- **Subscription Model**: $5–$10/month for new affirmations emailed weekly

Let's say you sell 100 printable affirmation packs a month at $10—that's $1,000 in digital income. Create seasonal or niche versions, and you can keep selling year-round.

Tips to Stand Out

- Use specific themes: "Affirmations for Moms Who Work from Home," "Christian Affirmations for Teens," "Morning Gratitude Cards"
- Offer bundles with journals, desktop wallpapers, or phone lock screens
- Include a free "sample card" set to get email sign-ups and grow your list
- Add usage ideas: "Pull one card each morning," or "Use these with your vision board"

16. Offer AI-Powered Course Outline and Curriculum Design Services

With online learning on the rise, everyone from entrepreneurs to professionals is looking to create and sell online courses. But here's the problem: many people don't know how to structure their content or even where to start. You can step in and offer a valuable, high-ticket service—using AI to help plan, organize, and outline complete course structures.

What You'll Do

You'll use AI tools like ChatGPT to help your clients transform their knowledge or ideas into structured course outlines and module breakdowns. You're not writing full video scripts (unless you want to upsell that too)—you're helping them get organized and ready to record.

Start by asking your client what their course is about, who it's for, and what outcome they want the student to achieve. Then use AI to generate:

- A course title and subtitle
- Learning objectives
- Module and lesson titles
- Key talking points for each lesson
- Suggested activities or quizzes
- Bonus ideas (checklists, PDFs, templates, etc.)

Example prompt:

"Create a 6-module course outline for a beginner-level online course about building a personal brand on social media. Include lesson titles, objectives, and content points for each."

ChatGPT returns a complete layout that your client can use to record videos, write materials, or build on later.

Why It Works

Most aspiring course creators get stuck at the planning phase. They have the knowledge, but no roadmap. Your service removes the overwhelm and gives them a clear path to launch—fast.

Because the value is high (you're helping them create something they can sell for years), you can charge more than other AI-powered services. And since AI does 70–80% of the work, your time stays efficient and your profits stay high.

Where to Find Clients

- **Coaches, Consultants, and Experts**: Reach out on Instagram, LinkedIn, or Facebook.
- **Fiverr & Upwork**: Offer "Online Course Outline Creation" or "Curriculum Planning for Digital Courses."
- **Facebook Groups**: Search for groups on course creation, Kajabi, Teachable, or Thinkific.
- **Podcasters & YouTubers**: Many have valuable content and want to repurpose it into a course.

What You'll Need

- ChatGPT (or similar) to generate the curriculum framework
- Google Docs or Notion to deliver and organize course plans
- Optional: Canva or PowerPoint if you want to offer slide deck outlines as a bonus
- A good intake form to gather what your client wants to teach

How Much You Can Charge

- **Basic Outline**: $100–$250 for a full 4–6 module breakdown
- **Full Curriculum Pack**: $300–$600+ including bonus material ideas and lesson development
- **Ongoing Retainers**: Offer content support or script writing for future modules

Even just 3–4 clients a month at $300 each brings in $900–$1,200/month with work you can complete in 1–2 hours per client.

Tips to Stand Out

- Specialize in a niche: "Course planning for fitness coaches," "Curriculum design for faith-based programs," or "Mini-course creation for social media experts."
- Include bonus tools: a course workbook template, lead magnet idea list, or launch strategy checklist.
- Offer a free call or sample module outline to attract new leads.
- Upsell a "Course-to-Ebook" version or "Turn Your Course Into a Scripted Podcast" add-on.

17. Create AI-Powered Quiz Funnels for Coaches and Online Businesses

Interactive quizzes have become one of the most powerful tools in digital marketing. Why? Because people love to answer questions about themselves—and businesses love the leads they generate. With AI, you can create personalized quiz funnels for coaches, course creators, or service providers that help them attract leads and sell their products—all without the client needing to lift a finger.

What You'll Do

You'll use AI to help brainstorm and write:

- Quiz titles and angles
- Engaging quiz questions (usually 5–10 per quiz)
- Personality-based or result-driven outcomes
- Email opt-in messages
- Follow-up email sequences
- Call-to-actions for offers or content upgrades

Example prompt:
"Create a 7-question quiz for a business coach called 'What's Your Entrepreneurial Superpower?' Include 4 possible outcomes and email opt-in copy."
AI will give you the entire structure—questions, answers, outcome descriptions, and even emails. You simply package it nicely in a Google Doc, or plug it into a quiz-building platform like:

- **Interact**
- **TryQuiz**
- **Typeform**
- **Thrive Quiz Builder (WordPress)**

This gives your client a done-for-you funnel they can use to generate leads or segment their email list.

Why It Works

Quiz funnels work because they're fun, personalized, and highly effective at turning cold traffic into subscribers. Coaches and digital product creators often want to use quizzes, but they don't know where to start. That's where your AI-backed service becomes a valuable shortcut.

And since the quiz leads directly to an offer, your client sees a clear return on investment—making this one of the higher-value services you can offer with AI support.

Where to Find Clients

- **Instagram Coaches and Service Providers**: Reach out and offer a lead generation quiz tailored to their niche.
- **Course Creators**: Look for those with a course but no entry funnel.
- **Fiverr or Upwork**: List your gig as "Custom Quiz Funnel Creation to Grow Your Email List or Sales."
- **Marketing Facebook Groups**: Coaches and funnel builders are constantly asking for quiz help.

What You'll Need

- ChatGPT or similar to generate quiz content and email copy
- Google Docs or Notion to deliver structured quiz plans
- (Optional) Experience with quiz platforms to offer full integration as an add-on

How Much You Can Charge

- **Basic Quiz Plan**: $100–$200 for quiz copy, outcomes, and opt-in messaging
- **Full Quiz Funnel**: $300–$600 including follow-up emails and platform setup
- **Retainer Offers**: $750–$1,000/month for lead magnet development plus funnel writing

Even with 2 full clients per month at $500, you're making $1,000/month from quiz creation—and each one can be done in just a few hours with AI.

Tips to Stand Out

- Offer niche-specific quizzes: "What Type of Real Estate Investor Are You?" or "Find Your Parenting Style in 5 Minutes"
- Include a bonus: list of email subject lines or a lead magnet that complements the quiz
- Show samples: create a mock quiz and display the outcomes visually in a Google Doc
- Partner with email marketers or funnel builders—they can refer quiz clients your way

18. Sell AI-Written eBooks on Amazon or Gumroad

eBooks are one of the most evergreen ways to earn passive income online—and with AI, you can create high-quality eBooks in a fraction of the time it would normally take. Whether you're writing fiction, non-fiction, how-to guides, devotionals, or niche-specific handbooks, AI helps you outline, write, edit, and publish with speed and ease.

What You'll Do

You'll use AI to generate content for complete eBooks, then format and sell them as Kindle eBooks on Amazon KDP, or as downloadable PDFs through Gumroad, Payhip, or your own site.

Your role will include:

- Choosing a niche or target audience
- Prompting ChatGPT to create the outline
- Expanding each section or chapter with additional prompts
- Editing or rewriting as needed
- Designing a simple cover and layout
- Uploading the final product for sale

Example prompts:

"Outline a 10-chapter eBook on how to build confidence as a teenage girl."

"Write a 1,000-word chapter on time management strategies for Christian entrepreneurs. Include scripture-based principles and practical examples."

With this approach, you could write an entire 10,000–15,000 word eBook in less than a week—even faster once you build your system.

Why It Works

People are always searching for information, inspiration, or entertainment they can read on their own time. eBooks are low-cost for readers and high-reward for creators. You write it once and it can sell for years.

Plus, AI eliminates the biggest pain point: the writing. Even if you're not a professional author, you can create a polished product by letting AI do the heavy lifting and using your voice to refine it.

You don't need a big following either—just a great title, niche topic, and a keyword-optimized description on Amazon or Gumroad.

Where to Sell

- **Amazon Kindle Direct Publishing (KDP)**: Great for mass exposure and royalties
- **Gumroad or Payhip**: Better for higher profits and direct audience building
- **Your Own Website**: Use your email list or social channels to drive sales
- **Bundles or Courses**: Offer the eBook as a lead magnet or bonus product

What You'll Need

- ChatGPT or similar AI writing tool
- Google Docs or Word for drafting
- Canva (free version works) for cover and interior design
- Amazon KDP or Gumroad account for publishing
- Optional: Grammarly for polishing your manuscript

How Much You Can Earn

- **Individual eBooks**: \$5–\$15 per sale (higher if bundled or sold with extra resources)
- **Royalties on Amazon KDP**: Up to 70% depending on price and region
- **Monthly Potential**: 100 sales at \$9 = \$900/month. Create multiple books and scale.

Some eBook sellers earn thousands per month by building a catalog of titles in different niches (health, faith, money, mindset, kids, etc.).

Tips to Stand Out

- Focus on *niche* audiences: "Devotional for Single Moms," "30-Day Fitness Plan for Busy Dads," "AI Tips for Etsy Sellers"
- Use clear, curiosity-driven titles and subtitle combinations
- Offer a free sample or lead magnet version to grow your email list
- Bundle multiple books for higher-ticket sales or limited-time offers

19. Start a Niche AI-Powered Blog and Monetize with Ads & Affiliates

Blogging isn't dead—it's just gotten smarter. With AI, you can build a content-rich niche blog faster than ever, populate it with SEO-optimized articles, and monetize through display ads, affiliate links, and digital product sales. It's a long-term play with passive income potential that grows over time.

What You'll Do

You'll create a blog in a specific niche (e.g., Christian finances, productivity for moms, AI for beginners, homeschooling tips, or plant-based recipes), then use AI to write and schedule articles regularly.
Start by identifying a niche you either know about or want to research.
Then use ChatGPT to:

- Brainstorm blog post ideas
- Create outlines and drafts
- Add SEO keywords
- Write product reviews, how-to guides, listicles, or comparison posts

Example prompt:
"Write a 1,000-word SEO blog post titled '7 Bible Verses Every Entrepreneur Should Know.' Use a friendly, devotional tone and include practical applications."
You can write 2–3 posts per week, schedule them in WordPress or a blogging platform like Ghost, and start promoting them via Pinterest, email, or SEO.

Why It Works

Blog traffic compounds over time. With the right keywords, your posts will bring in free organic visitors who read your content, click your links, or buy your products. AI makes it possible to publish 10x faster than traditional blogging—and without burning out from writing.
You're not just building a website—you're building a *digital asset* that can earn income every month through multiple channels:

- **Ads (Google AdSense, Ezoic, Mediavine)**
- **Affiliate links (Amazon, ShareASale, Impact)**
- **Digital products (printables, eBooks, mini-courses)**
- **Sponsored content**

Where to Promote Your Blog

- **Pinterest**: Best for lifestyle, parenting, wellness, and faith blogs
- **Facebook Groups**: Share relevant posts in niche communities
- **SEO (Google)**: Use free keyword tools like Ubersuggest or Keywords Everywhere
- **Email List**: Offer a freebie in exchange for email signups and nurture traffic long-term

What You'll Need

- ChatGPT for generating blog content
- WordPress, Ghost, or another blogging platform
- Canva for creating blog graphics and Pinterest pins
- Google Analytics or Search Console to track performance
- Optional: Grammarly or SurferSEO for refining content

How Much You Can Earn

- **Ads**: $5–$25 per 1,000 visitors (depending on your niche and ad platform)
- **Affiliate Links**: $100–$500+/month with well-placed product recommendations
- **Digital Products**: Add a $9–$29 product and earn even more
- **Total Monthly Potential**: $1,000–$5,000+ after 3–12 months of consistent work

The more high-quality content you post, the more your traffic—and income—grows. This method is scalable and sellable later (people buy monetized blogs for 30x monthly profit).

Tips to Stand Out

- Choose a niche with strong community and search potential
- Use content clusters (e.g., 10 related posts around "Christian business tips")
- Add personal stories or biblical references to make it more relatable
- Design your blog to be clean, easy to navigate, and mobile-friendly
- Offer a lead magnet (e.g., free devotional PDF, checklist, or journal prompt) to grow your list

20. Offer AI-Generated FAQ Pages and Help Docs for Websites

Every website needs an FAQ section and clear help documentation—but most business owners never get around to writing them. They either leave it blank, throw in a few basic questions, or copy and paste something generic. With AI, you can step in and offer a highly valuable service: writing detailed, brand-specific FAQ pages and help center articles that improve user experience, reduce support tickets, and boost SEO.

What You'll Do

You'll offer a service that creates comprehensive FAQ pages or help documents for businesses, coaches, course creators, and eCommerce brands. These can include:

- Frequently Asked Questions
- Troubleshooting guides
- Return/exchange policy explanations
- Onboarding steps for new customers
- "How it works" breakdowns

All you need is some basic info from your client:

- What they sell
- Common customer questions
- Any past support messages or inquiries
- Brand voice (formal, friendly, playful, etc.)

Then, prompt ChatGPT like this:

"Generate a 12-question FAQ section for an online course teaching digital marketing to beginners. Use a confident, encouraging tone."

"Write a help article explaining how to return a product to an eCommerce store that sells eco-friendly clothing."

You'll receive polished, customer-friendly content that can be lightly edited, formatted, and sent to your client for immediate use.

Why It Works

Clear communication reduces confusion, builds trust, and saves time. A strong FAQ or help section makes a site look more professional and decreases customer service workload. Business owners know this—but rarely have the time to write one that sounds good.

That's where your service stands out: it's quick, affordable, and makes an immediate difference to the business. Plus, help documentation improves SEO by answering long-tail questions that people search for.

Where to Find Clients

- **eCommerce Stores**: Especially those on Shopify, Etsy, or Wix
- **Course Creators**: Often need onboarding docs and refund FAQs
- **Coaches and Consultants**: They often get repeated questions in their DMs
- **Web Designers**: Partner with them to offer your FAQ service as an add-on
- **Fiverr & Upwork**: List your gig as "Website FAQ Page and Help Docs with AI-Powered Clarity"

What You'll Need

- ChatGPT or another AI writing assistant
- Google Docs for formatting the content
- Optional: Grammarly for final editing
- A simple intake form for collecting your client's brand info and FAQs

How Much You Can Charge

- **Basic FAQ Page (10–15 questions)**: $75–$150
- **Help Center Articles (per article)**: $50–$100
- **Full Support Pack**: $300–$600 for multiple help docs + FAQ section
- **White-Label Add-On**: Partner with agencies and get repeat business

Just 5 clients at $150 each = $750/month with minimal time commitment. Even better, many clients need *updates* or *additional sections* over time.

Tips to Stand Out

- Offer a "conversion-focused" FAQ strategy: helping turn visitors into buyers
- Provide examples of tone: "friendly," "formal," "tech-savvy," etc.
- Create templates or packages by niche (e.g., FAQs for course creators, Shopify stores, or Christian coaches)
- Upsell with policies, onboarding emails, or terms & conditions writing (also AI-supported)

21. Build and Sell AI-Generated Templates for Entrepreneurs

Templates are gold in the digital economy. Business owners, coaches, and content creators are constantly looking for tools that save them time and make them look professional. Whether it's email templates, landing page copy, social media bios, or business plans—you can use AI to create polished, plug-and-play templates and sell them over and over again.

What You'll Do

You'll use ChatGPT and Canva (or even Google Docs) to create ready-to-use templates that help your audience accomplish something specific—faster.

Popular AI-powered template ideas:

- Welcome email sequences for coaches
- Sales page copy templates
- Client onboarding questionnaires
- Social media bio templates (Instagram, TikTok, LinkedIn)
- Vision statement or mission statement templates
- Weekly content planning templates
- Christian business devotionals with fill-in-the-blanks

Example prompt:

"Write a customizable email template for a life coach welcoming a new client, with fields for name, coaching goals, and session times."

You can even turn one AI-generated sample into 3–5 variations (for different industries, tones, or platforms), then bundle them together and sell them as a toolkit.

Why It Works

Time is money. Entrepreneurs and solopreneurs want shortcuts that still look and sound great. Templates remove the overwhelm of starting from scratch and give them a foundation to customize and launch quickly.

Your AI-powered templates help them launch websites, market their services, and onboard clients with confidence. Since they're digital, you create them once and sell forever.

This also works well as a niche passive income product—you don't need a big audience to earn consistently from templates.

Where to Sell or Promote

Etsy: Great for PDF or Canva template packs

- **Gumroad or Payhip**: Sell your bundles and allow instant downloads
- **Your Own Website**: Build a shop or landing page and grow an email list
- **Pinterest or TikTok**: Post template demos, mockups, or use cases to drive traffic

What You'll Need

- ChatGPT to write content or copy sections
- Canva or Google Docs to format and brand your templates
- Etsy, Gumroad, Payhip, or Shopify to sell
- Optional: Use ThriveCart or ConvertKit if you want to offer upsells or email automation

How Much You Can Charge

- **Single Templates**: $5–$15
- **Bundles**: $20–$50+
- **Premium Packs**: $75–$150 for fully branded toolkits or business bundles
- **Subscription Model**: Offer 5 new templates/month for $9.99–$19.99

Let's say you sell 100 template packs a month at $25 each—that's $2,500 in digital product income, with no inventory and little to no ongoing work.

Tips to Stand Out

- Niche down: "Templates for Christian Coaches," "Email Templates for Etsy Sellers," "Bios for Fitness Influencers"
- Add bonus guides: a 1-page PDF on "How to Use These Templates for Best Results"
- Use mockups in your listings to make the templates look polished and professional
- Include both editable versions (Canva/Google Docs) and PDFs for different buyer preferences

22. Start a Done-for-You AI LinkedIn Profile Optimization Service

LinkedIn has become one of the top platforms for networking, hiring, and building personal brands. But most people still have weak, outdated, or poorly written profiles. With AI, you can offer a done-for-you LinkedIn optimization service—helping professionals stand out, attract recruiters, or grow their authority in their industry.

What You'll Do

You'll use AI to rewrite and optimize key sections of a LinkedIn profile:

- Headline (the short bio under the name)
- About/Summary section
- Experience descriptions
- Skills section
- Featured content or call to action

With just a few details from your client (job title, industry, goals, tone), you can prompt ChatGPT like this:

"Write a compelling LinkedIn summary for a mid-level software engineer looking to pivot into product management. Make it confident, personable, and goal-oriented."

Or:

"Create 3 LinkedIn headline options for a Christian business coach helping faith-based entrepreneurs grow online."

You'll then clean up the output, ensure it's keyword-optimized, and deliver a fully revamped profile—or offer to walk the client through the changes.

Why It Works

LinkedIn is one of the few places where professionals actively *want* to improve how they're perceived online—but most don't know how. A strong profile can lead to job offers, speaking gigs, or coaching clients. Your service becomes a career upgrade—and with AI, it only takes you a fraction of the time it would normally take a traditional resume writer.

You can even bundle this with resume/cover letter services (#1 on your list), making it a perfect complementary offer.

Where to Find Clients

- **Job Seekers**: Especially mid-career professionals or recent graduates
- **Coaches & Consultants**: Want their profile to reflect their brand
- **Freelancers & Creators**: Need better bios to attract high-paying clients
- **LinkedIn & Upwork**: Offer your service directly on the platforms where your audience already is
- **Facebook Groups & Instagram DMs**: Great for targeting coaches or creators who haven't updated their profiles in months

What You'll Need

- ChatGPT to write and improve profile sections
- Google Docs or Notion to deliver drafts and alternate options
- A short intake form or onboarding questionnaire (to understand the client's tone, goal, and background)
- Optional: Grammarly for polishing the final copy

How Much You Can Charge

- **Profile Rewrite Only**: $75–$150
- **Full Optimization Package**: $200–$400 (includes headline, summary, experience section rewrites, and keyword strategy)
- **Add-On Services**: LinkedIn content strategy, connection messaging templates, or resume/CV revamp

Even with just 4 full-package clients at $300/month = $1,200/month, and the work can be done in a day or two per profile.

Tips to Stand Out

- Offer before/after examples of real profiles (with permission)
- Create a short portfolio with headline options and summary transformations
- Add "LinkedIn Optimization for [Specific Niche]" like tech pros, freelancers, or faith-based entrepreneurs
- Include a quick-win freebie, like "5 LinkedIn Headline Templates to Instantly Stand Out," to grow an email list or warm up leads

23. Create AI-Generated Devotionals and Sell Them as Digital Products

Devotionals are a timeless resource in the faith-based community. People crave short, daily encouragements rooted in scripture that speak to real-life situations. With AI, you can create beautiful, thoughtful, and relevant devotionals that resonate with a specific audience—and sell them as digital downloads, email series, or printables.

What You'll Do

You'll use AI to generate a set of devotionals around a central theme, such as:

- Healing from trauma
- Faith and entrepreneurship
- Overcoming fear
- Identity in Christ
- Prayers for busy moms
- Daily wisdom for teens

Each devotional can include:

- A short scripture
- A 150–300 word reflection or encouragement
- A prayer or call to action
- Optional journaling prompts

Example prompt:

"Create 30 daily devotionals for women going through a difficult season. Each should include a Bible verse, a short reflection (200 words), and a one-sentence prayer."

With one solid prompt, you can generate a full 30-day devotional book in a day. Add your personal touches or edits, then format it into a clean PDF using Canva, Google Docs, or PowerPoint.

You can sell it as:

- A downloadable eBook
- A printable devotional journal
- An email-based devotional challenge (one email per day for 30 days)
- A bonus in a Christian course or coaching program

Why It Works

Faith-based audiences are deeply connected to written encouragement—especially when it's personal, relatable, and biblically rooted. But many people don't have the time, skills, or confidence to write their own devotional materials. Your service or product provides spiritual nourishment in a format they can engage with daily. Plus, devotionals are evergreen. Once created, they can sell again and again. They also pair perfectly with email opt-ins, sermon bundles, or themed journals.

Where to Sell or Promote

- **Etsy**: Ideal for devotional journals, printables, or PDF bundles
- **Gumroad or Payhip**: Easy setup for downloadable eBooks and recurring sales
- **Your Own Website**: Use for content marketing, lead generation, or as part of a Christian entrepreneur platform
- **Email List**: Offer a free 7-day devotional to grow your list, then upsell the full 30-day version
- **Facebook Groups & Pinterest**: Both are huge platforms for Christian women and faith-based resources

What You'll Need

- ChatGPT for writing the devotionals
- Canva or Word for formatting
- Etsy, Gumroad, or your website for distribution
- Optional: ConvertKit or Mailchimp to send daily devotionals by email
- Optional: A printable journal version (just add journaling prompts and spacing)

How Much You Can Charge

- **Single Devotional eBooks**: $5–$15
- **Themed Bundles or Printables**: $20–$35
- **Email-Based Devotional Series**: $9–$29 for access
- **Upsell Products**: Journals, prayer cards, scripture coloring pages, or courses

You only need to sell 100 copies at $10 to bring in $1,000—and if you create a few niche-specific versions, this becomes a serious passive income source.

Tips to Stand Out

- Choose specific audiences: "Devotionals for First-Time Moms," "Faith in the Workplace," "Healing After Loss"
- Include reflection questions or journaling prompts to deepen the reader's connection
- Pair your devotional with a matching digital journal or wall art print
- Turn one devotional set into multiple products (email series, printable, podcast audio, etc.)

24. Start an AI-Powered Scriptwriting Service for Voiceovers and Audiobooks

With the rise of YouTube narrations, TikTok voiceovers, podcast intros, and self-published audiobooks, demand for high-quality voiceover scripts is exploding. The problem? Most people aren't great at writing spoken-word content that flows naturally. You can fill that gap with an AI-powered voiceover scriptwriting service.

What You'll Do

You'll offer customized, ready-to-record scripts for creators, voiceover artists, podcasters, or audiobook publishers using AI tools like ChatGPT. You'll specialize in writing copy that sounds *spoken*—not stiff or robotic—and is formatted for easy reading in voiceovers.

Types of scripts you can create:

- YouTube narration scripts
- Podcast intros/outros
- Voiceovers for short-form videos (TikTok, Instagram Reels)
- Commercial ad reads or promo voiceovers
- Short audiobook chapters or devotionals

Start by gathering basic details from your client:

- Tone and style (fun, corporate, spiritual, dramatic, etc.)
- Target audience
- Purpose (entertainment, education, promotion)
- Desired length

Example prompt:

"Write a 3-minute voiceover script for a motivational TikTok channel about not giving up after failure. Use an energetic, uplifting tone and end with a powerful one-liner."

Or:

"Create a 5-minute voiceover script for a Christian audiobook devotional about finding peace in hard times. Include scripture, a short reflection, and a prayer."

You format and polish the AI-generated script, making sure it flows naturally when spoken.

Why It Works

More creators are turning to voice-driven content—but they don't want to spend hours writing scripts, or worse, wing it and sound

unprepared. A great script increases engagement, professionalism, and listener retention.

You're not just helping them sound better—you're saving them time and giving them confidence behind the mic.

Where to Find Clients

- **YouTubers & Podcasters**: Especially smaller creators looking to scale
- **TikTok & Reels Creators**: Voiceover scripts for short motivational or educational content
- **Fiverr & Upwork**: Offer "Voiceover Scriptwriting" for different lengths and platforms
- **Christian Creators or Authors**: Many need help writing audiobook devotionals, prayer readings, or intros
- **Voiceover Artists**: Many of them need original scripts to demo or sell with their service

What You'll Need

- ChatGPT to write and refine scripts
- Google Docs or Notion to format and deliver
- Optional: Grammarly or Hemingway for clarity and rhythm
- Optional: A free voice recorder or text-to-speech tool to test how your script sounds when read aloud

How Much You Can Charge

- **Short Scripts (1–2 mins)**: $25–$50
- **Medium Scripts (3–5 mins)**: $75–$150
- **Long-Form Narration (10+ mins or chapters)**: $200–$400+
- **Bundles**: Sell script packs for $250–$500

Just five short scripts a week at $50 = $1,000/month. And if you add editing, consulting, or delivery formatting, you can increase your fees significantly.

Tips to Stand Out

- Offer sample script snippets in your portfolio—show different tones and niches
- Learn to format scripts with clear breaks, pacing, and emphasis (voiceover pros will love this)
- Upsell script + storyboard + video idea combo packs for content creators
- Niche down: "Scripts for Christian voiceovers," "Motivational TikTok script packs," "Audiobook devotionals for self-publishers"

25. Offer AI-Based Business Naming and Branding Ideas as a Service

Every new business, product, or brand needs a name—and coming up with the *right* one is often one of the hardest, most stressful parts of launching. That's where your service comes in. Using AI, you can generate creative, relevant, and niche-specific business names, taglines, and brand ideas for entrepreneurs, creators, and startups—and charge for it.

What You'll Do

You'll use AI tools like ChatGPT to brainstorm:

- Business names
- Product names
- Brand taglines or slogans
- Domain name suggestions
- Instagram handles or TikTok usernames
- Podcast or YouTube channel names

Your client gives you basic info about their brand—what they do, who they serve, and their desired vibe (fun, luxury, spiritual, bold, etc.).

Then you feed prompts like this to AI:

"Give me 20 brand name ideas for a Christian-based fitness coaching business for women. Include a mix of playful and powerful options. Also suggest Instagram handle ideas."

Or:

"Suggest 15 podcast name ideas for a show about overcoming addiction and finding purpose in life. Include subtitle/tagline options for each."

AI will give you a full list of ideas in seconds. You can then refine, organize, and deliver it as a professional naming package.

Why It Works

A good name sets the tone for the entire business. But most people struggle to create something unique, memorable, and available online. Your AI-enhanced naming service removes that pain point—fast.

It's also an emotional service: when you help someone find *the* perfect name for their dream business or passion project, they're thankful—and likely to refer others.

You can even bundle it with logo design (using Canva or Canva Pro), social media bio writing, or domain setup support.

Where to Find Clients

- **New Entrepreneurs**: Especially on Instagram, TikTok, or in Facebook Groups
- **Freelancers or Coaches**: Rebranding or launching new services
- **Etsy or Shopify Sellers**: Launching new product lines or shops
- **Fiverr & Upwork**: Offer "Business Naming Packages" or "Brand Identity Starter Kits"
- **Startup Forums & Side Hustle Communities**: Reddit, Indie Hackers, etc.

What You'll Need

- ChatGPT or any AI text generation tool
- Google Docs or Canva for formatting and branding presentation
- Optional: Domain checker tools (Namecheap, GoDaddy) to confirm name availability
- Optional: Canva for a logo or brand mood board add-on

How Much You Can Charge

- **Basic Naming Package**: \$50–\$100 (10–20 name options + tagline ideas)
- **Premium Brand Kit**: \$200–\$500 (names, taglines, logo, brand story, colors, fonts, IG bio)
- **Recurring Offers**: Bundle naming services with brand coaching or design retainers

Five clients at \$150 = \$750/month—and once you get known for great names, referrals come fast.

Tips to Stand Out

- Offer naming by niche: "Faith-based business names," "Names for women-owned product brands," or "Podcast name ideas for coaches"
- Share before/after examples in your portfolio
- Offer a freebie: "15 Christian Business Name Ideas to Inspire You" as a lead magnet
- Include social media handle availability in your packages (big plus!)

26. Sell AI-Created Lead Magnets to Coaches and Course Creators

Lead magnets are the lifeblood of online business. Every coach, content creator, or service provider needs a compelling freebie to grow their email list—but most either don't have time to create one, or struggle to make it sound valuable. With AI, you can create done-for-you lead magnets fast and sell them as a service or digital product.

What You'll Do

You'll offer lead magnet creation packages using AI to generate:

- eBooks and guides (5–10 pages)
- Checklists and cheat sheets
- Swipe files or templates
- Mini-devotionals or affirmations
- Quick-start roadmaps or challenges

Example prompt:
"Write a 5-page guide titled '7 Ways Christian Entrepreneurs Can Hear God More Clearly in Business.' Include tips, scripture references, and a call to action."
Or:
"Create a printable checklist for new coaches launching their first email list. Include 15 clear steps and quick descriptions."
Once AI gives you the content, you'll polish it and format it into a visually appealing PDF using **Canva**. Then, deliver it to your client or sell it as a template others can customize and use.
You can offer this as:

- A custom DFY service for one-on-one clients
- Pre-written, editable templates for sale on Gumroad or Etsy
- A side hustle that turns into a passive product line

Why It Works

Every business with an email list needs a freebie to entice signups—but most people get stuck figuring out what to offer, or how to create it. Your service solves *both* problems: idea + creation.
Lead magnets are also high-value assets. They help clients build their audience, increase conversions, and set up future sales funnels. Since AI helps you do it quickly, your margins stay high.

Where to Find Clients

- **Coaches and Course Creators**: They often post asking for lead magnet help in groups or on IG
- **Facebook Groups for Online Businesses**: Offer free tips and drop your service link
- **Fiverr & Upwork**: List "Lead Magnet Design & Copywriting for Coaches"
- **Email Marketers**: They often outsource the content creation for their clients
- **Instagram & TikTok**: DM small creators with audience growth goals

What You'll Need

- ChatGPT (or similar AI) to write and outline content
- Canva or Google Docs for formatting and design
- Gumroad or Payhip if selling ready-made templates
- Optional: ConvertKit or MailerLite knowledge if helping clients connect the freebie to their email system

How Much You Can Charge

- **Custom Lead Magnet (5–7 pages)**: $100–$250
- **Done-for-You Bundle (magnet + landing page copy)**: $300–$600+
- **Editable Template Packs**: $20–$50 each
- **Monthly Income**: 4 DFY clients/month at $200 = $800. Passive template sales = extra $500–$1,000+

You can also use this as an upsell or lead-in to other services like full funnel setup or email sequences.

Tips to Stand Out

- Offer niche options: "Lead Magnets for Christian Coaches," "Checklists for Real Estate Pros," "Mini Guides for Wellness Brands"
- Include editable Canva files so clients can tweak them later
- Offer to add CTAs, social links, or email list signup instructions
- Create a "Lead Magnet Starter Kit" bundle as a passive income product

27. Start an AI-Generated Daily Quote or Scripture Subscription Service

People crave daily encouragement—especially when it comes from a source that aligns with their values, goals, or faith. With AI, you can easily create daily quote or scripture packs and offer them as a subscription service. Whether it's sent through email, text, or a private app, you can deliver consistent inspiration and get paid for it monthly.

What You'll Do

You'll use AI to generate:

- Daily motivational quotes
- Christian scriptures with reflections
- Affirmations or declarations
- Morning devotionals or journal prompts

Then you'll organize and automate delivery in one of several formats:

- Email (via MailerLite, ConvertKit, or Substack)
- Text message (via platforms like Community, Project Broadcast, or SlickText)
- A downloadable monthly calendar
- Private access through a paid Telegram or Facebook group

Example AI prompt:

"Create 31 daily Bible verses with short 2-sentence reflections for Christian entrepreneurs focused on purpose, provision, and perseverance."

Or:

"Write 30 motivational quotes for women who are rebuilding confidence after a breakup. Include 5-word affirmation options for each quote."

You can pre-create content in monthly batches, then schedule it in advance—making this an ideal recurring revenue model.

Why It Works

People love bite-sized inspiration. And they *pay* for it when it's:

- Personalized to their season or identity (e.g., moms, faith-driven founders, men overcoming addiction)
- Conveniently delivered (email or phone)
- Professionally packaged (formatted clean, beautifully designed, or curated)

This model creates predictable income, builds trust with your audience, and positions you as a thought leader or encourager in your niche.

Where to Sell or Promote

- **Instagram or TikTok**: Share sample quotes and drive followers to your sign-up link
- **Facebook Groups**: Post themed samples that speak to your niche
- **Gumroad or Payhip**: Offer monthly quote packs as a download
- **Your Website or Email List**: Turn this into a recurring product or freebie-to-paid upsell

What You'll Need

- ChatGPT to generate quotes, scriptures, or affirmations
- Canva (optional) to design daily cards or quote graphics
- ConvertKit, MailerLite, or Substack to manage delivery
- Gumroad or Payhip if offering static packs instead of subscriptions

How Much You Can Charge

- **Monthly Email/Text Service**: \$5–\$15/month
- **Annual Access**: \$49–\$99/year
- **Downloadable Packs**: \$7–\$20 per themed collection (e.g., "31 Scriptures for Healing")
- **Private Group Access**: \$10–\$25/month for community + content delivery

100 subscribers paying \$10/month = \$1,000/month in recurring revenue. And with content batch-created via AI, your workload stays light.

Tips to Stand Out

- Offer themed tracks: "Confidence Quotes for Christian Women," "Morning Scriptures for Founders," or "Motivational Messages for Teens"
- Use carousel posts or reels to showcase sample content
- Offer the first 7 days free as a teaser
- Bundle printable calendars, journals, or wallpapers with your subscription

28. Offer AI-Powered Social Media Bio Optimization Services

Your social media bio is your elevator pitch—it tells visitors who you are, what you do, and why they should follow you. But most people either overthink it or throw something together last-minute. With AI, you can create optimized bios for Instagram, TikTok, YouTube, LinkedIn, and Twitter that help users grow their brand, increase clicks, and attract ideal followers or clients.

What You'll Do

You'll offer a service where you take someone's current social media bio and upgrade it using AI. Or, you create a new one from scratch based on who they are and what they want to achieve.

Bios you can write:

- Instagram or TikTok bio (150 characters)
- YouTube channel "About" section
- LinkedIn tagline + summary
- Twitter bio (160 characters)
- Link-in-bio headlines or micro-descriptions

You'll ask the client for a few key details:

- Who they are (coach, influencer, small biz, etc.)
- Who they serve
- Tone they want (funny, professional, inspiring, spiritual, bold)
- CTA (book a call, visit website, shop now, etc.)

Sample AI prompt:

"Write 5 Instagram bios for a Christian relationship coach helping women prepare for godly marriages. Use a warm and empowering tone. Include a CTA."

Or:

"Rewrite this LinkedIn bio to be more engaging and concise for a digital marketer targeting real estate agents."

You'll clean up the AI output and format multiple variations for the client to choose from.

Why It Works

Social bios are short but powerful. They're often the first thing someone reads before clicking "follow" or "book a call." Most people know theirs needs work but don't know how to fix it—and they're willing to pay a small fee for something that could drastically improve their conversions and credibility.

You can also turn this into a rapid-fire service, since it takes less than 30 minutes to deliver with the right system.

Where to Find Clients

- **Instagram & TikTok Creators**: DM small business owners or new influencers
- **Facebook Groups**: Offer free critiques and upsell the service
- **Fiverr & Upwork**: List a gig like "Bio Writing for Instagram, LinkedIn & More"
- **LinkedIn**: Especially for job seekers, coaches, and consultants
- **DM Coaches and Creators**: Offer a free bio audit or "first draft free"

What You'll Need

- ChatGPT for rapid generation
- Google Docs or Notion for delivery
- Optional: Canva to create stylized versions or mockups
- Optional: Intake form (Google Form or Typeform) for easy client info collection

How Much You Can Charge

- **Single Bio Revamp**: \$25–\$75
- **Platform Bundle (3–5 bios)**: \$100–\$200
- **Add-On Packages**: Include hashtag strategy, link-in-bio wording, or profile pic feedback

5 clients per week at \$50 = \$1,000/month. And once you build a portfolio, it's a fast and scalable service.

Tips to Stand Out

- Niche down: "Bios for Coaches," "Christian Creators," or "Real Estate Influencers"
- Offer a "before and after" bio preview
- Include CTA examples tailored to platforms (e.g., "📩 DM me to start," or "👇 Grab your free guide")
- Turn this into a *bio + content pillars* mini service to boost perceived value

29. Use AI to Build and Sell Digital Vision Board Kits

Vision boards aren't just pretty collages—they're powerful tools that help people visualize and work toward their goals. With AI, you can quickly generate affirmations, goal prompts, themed images, and motivational phrases to create **digital vision board kits** you can sell as downloads or use as part of a coaching or goal-setting program.

What You'll Do

You'll create complete vision board kits around specific themes or audiences, using AI to generate the **inspirational words**, **goals**, **affirmations**, and **categories** people want to include.

Types of kits:

- Personal growth vision board (mind, body, spirit)
- Christian vision board kit (faith, purpose, family)
- Wealth & abundance kit (financial goals, affirmations, success)
- Relationship & marriage vision boards
- Business owner or entrepreneur-focused boards

Prompt examples:

"Generate 50 motivational words and short affirmations for a Christian woman building her dream life. Include faith, family, business, and health themes."

"List 20 future-based goals and vision statements for a digital entrepreneur in their 20s."

You'll take the AI-generated content and format it into a beautiful Canva or PDF template with:

- Cut-and-paste phrases
- Affirmation cards
- Goal-setting worksheets
- Optional blank space for personal visuals
- Print-at-home or drag-and-drop vision board tools

You can sell this as a standalone product or a bonus resource for coaches and digital product sellers.

Why It Works

Vision boards are highly personal and emotional—and people love products that help them dream, plan, and stay focused. But not everyone knows how to make one or what to include.

You're selling **a shortcut to clarity** with structure, words, and visuals already prepared. And since the content is mostly evergreen, you can sell it over and over again as a passive product.
This is perfect for:

- Etsy
- Gumroad
- Your coaching website
- Bundles with journals or devotionals

Where to Sell or Promote

- **Etsy**: One of the top platforms for digital planners, printables, and vision board kits
- **Gumroad or Payhip**: Simple storefront for passive income
- **Pinterest**: Huge traffic source for vision board and goal-setting content
- **Instagram Reels or TikTok**: Show "What's Inside My Vision Board Kit" videos
- **Email List or Website**: Offer as a bonus for subscribers or coaching clients

What You'll Need

- ChatGPT to generate the words, affirmations, and ideas
- Canva to design the kit (with print or drag-and-drop options)
- Gumroad, Etsy, or your own site to sell
- Optional: Trello or Notion templates if you want to create digital vision boards

How Much You Can Charge

- **Printable Kits**: \$7–\$15
- **Deluxe Bundles**: \$20–\$35 (includes planner, goal-setting workbook, wallpapers)
- **Custom Kits**: \$50–\$100+ (if you offer personalization for coaches or events)

If you sell 200 kits at \$15, that's \$3,000—with a product you built once using AI.

Tips to Stand Out

- Focus on niche kits: "Christian Entrepreneur Vision Board," "Teen Girl Confidence Kit," "2025 Faith & Finance Vision Kit"
- Use mockups that show printed pages, scissors, and cut-outs to trigger the crafting vibe
- Offer matching wallpaper packs or desktop versions as upsells
- Include QR codes to motivational playlists, prayers, or meditations

30. Use AI to Write and Sell Mini Email Courses

Mini email courses are a brilliant way to teach, nurture, and convert your audience—all on autopilot. With AI, you can write entire multi-day email courses in a matter of hours, then either sell them as digital products, offer them as lead magnets, or build them out for other businesses as a service.

What You'll Do

You'll use ChatGPT to outline, write, and structure 3- to 7-day email courses for specific niches. These short courses deliver daily lessons, insights, or tips directly to the subscriber's inbox.

Popular course topics include:

- "5 Days to Start Your Etsy Shop"
- "7 Days to Reset Your Mindset with Scripture"
- "How to Grow Your Email List in 5 Days"
- "The Christian Entrepreneur's Confidence Challenge"
- "Launch Your First Digital Product in 7 Steps"

Example AI prompt:

"Write a 5-day email course called 'Faith Over Fear: A Christian's Guide to Taking Bold Action.' Each email should include a scripture, a short teaching, and a simple daily challenge."

Or:

"Create a 7-day email course for new freelancers learning how to find clients. Each email should include 1 key lesson and an action step."

Once AI gives you the raw emails, you polish them up, format for delivery, and either:

- Sell the course as a product on Gumroad or Payhip
- Offer it as a lead magnet to build your email list
- Create it for clients who want their own automated nurture sequence

Why It Works

Email courses feel personal and valuable—but they're 100% automated once set up. People love short, results-focused learning delivered over a few days. Coaches, creators, and business owners love using them to sell higher-ticket offers.

And since AI can create the bulk of the content, you can launch multiple mini-courses fast—or offer it as a writing service with high perceived value.

Where to Sell or Use It

- **Gumroad or Payhip**: Sell as a low-ticket course product
- **ConvertKit, MailerLite, or Flodesk**: Deliver the course automatically
- **Etsy**: List email course templates or planners
- **Your Own Website**: Use as a lead magnet or tripwire product
- **Offer as a Service**: Write branded email courses for coaches, consultants, or service providers

What You'll Need

- ChatGPT to generate and outline email sequences
- ConvertKit, MailerLite, or Substack to automate email delivery
- Google Docs to format and edit
- Optional: Canva if you want to include bonus downloads or branded PDFs

How Much You Can Charge or Earn

- **Selling a Mini Course**: $9–$29 as a product
- **Writing for Clients**: $150–$500 per course (5–7 emails + CTA)
- **Lead Magnet Model**: Use it to grow an email list and sell backend products or services
- **Bundle Packs**: $100+ for themed course bundles

If you sell 100 mini email courses at $19, that's $1,900 with automated delivery—and if you offer it as a service, 4 clients/month at $250 is $1,000.

Tips to Stand Out

- Theme your courses for specific identities: "Email Course for Christian Creatives," "Confidence Bootcamp for Teen Girls," or "Freelancer Fast Track"
- Offer matching PDF journals or bonus printables to increase value
- Use a countdown CTA in the final email to upsell a digital product or consultation
- Build a collection: 3–5 mini courses in different niches = multiple income streams

31. Create and Sell AI-Generated "Done-for-You" Content Calendars

Content is king—but consistent content is hard. Business owners, influencers, and coaches constantly struggle with *what to post* each day. That's where your AI-powered content calendar service comes in. You'll provide ready-to-use monthly or weekly content plans that help people stay consistent and grow their audience—without the stress.

What You'll Do

You'll use AI to create niche-specific content calendars filled with:

- Daily post ideas
- Captions or prompts
- Hashtag suggestions
- Call-to-actions
- Content themes for each week or day

These calendars can be delivered as:

- PDFs (printable or viewable)
- Editable Google Sheets or Notion templates
- Canva-designed planners
- Bonus tools in digital marketing courses or bundles

Example AI prompt:

"Create a 30-day content calendar for a Christian life coach on Instagram. Include daily post ideas, scripture-based themes, and one weekly reel suggestion."

Or:

"Build a 4-week TikTok content calendar for a personal finance creator. Include hook ideas, trending themes, and money-saving tips."

Once AI gives you the content, you format it beautifully and sell it as a digital product—or offer it as a service for custom requests.

Why It Works

Content creation is overwhelming for most people. They want consistency without having to sit down and plan it themselves. Your calendar gives them structure, saves them hours each month, and keeps their audience engaged.

Even better: once created, these calendars become passive products you can sell again and again—or use to land recurring clients who want *fresh content monthly.*

Where to Sell or Promote

- **Etsy**: Perfect for digital planners and content calendars
- **Gumroad or Payhip**: Easy to sell one-off or bundle products
- **Instagram or TikTok**: Show your calendars in action with behind-the-scenes reels or carousel previews
- **Facebook Groups**: Creators, coaches, and small biz owners LOVE done-for-you tools
- **Fiverr or Upwork**: Offer custom calendars as a gig or retainer service

What You'll Need

- ChatGPT to generate daily prompts, ideas, hashtags, and themes
- Canva or Google Sheets to format the calendars
- Etsy, Gumroad, or your own site to sell
- Optional: Trello or Notion if offering digital calendar boards

How Much You Can Charge

- **Monthly Calendars**: $10–$25
- **Niche Bundles (3 months or more)**: $35–$75
- **Custom Calendars (for clients)**: $100–$300
- **Recurring Retainer**: $200–$500/month for done-for-you content planning

Even with just 50 people buying a $20 calendar = $1,000. Add 3 monthly clients at $300 each = $900/month recurring.

Tips to Stand Out

- Niche your calendars: "Content Calendar for Christian Coaches," "TikTok for Skincare Brands," "Instagram for Etsy Shops"
- Offer 7-day sample calendars as lead magnets
- Include Canva caption templates, carousel outlines, or reel scripts for extra value
- Add a "blank calendar" version so clients can customize and reuse

32. Launch a Niche AI-Powered Podcast Idea Generator + Episode Planner

Podcasts are booming, but one of the biggest struggles for podcasters is consistently coming up with fresh, relevant, and engaging episode ideas. With AI, you can offer a service (or product) that generates **custom podcast episode topics**, outlines, and even titles—either on demand or delivered as monthly content plans.

What You'll Do

You'll use AI to brainstorm:

- Podcast episode titles
- Content themes
- Weekly or monthly topic outlines
- Guest question ideas
- Show notes and descriptions
- Episode scripts or intro/outro ideas (optional upsell)

You can deliver this as:

- A one-time "50 episode ideas" package
- Monthly podcast content calendars
- Done-for-you outlines with talking points
- Customized packages based on niche and tone

Example AI prompt:

"Create 20 podcast episode titles for a Christian entrepreneur helping women step into their purpose. Make them sound motivational and spiritually grounded."

Or:

"Build a 4-week podcast content plan for a show about budgeting and financial literacy for single moms. Include episode titles, bullet-point outlines, and show notes."

Once generated, you'll clean up the language, organize it by category or theme, and package it into a document or planner.

Why It Works

Podcasters are content machines—but the planning part is where many hit a wall. They want to focus on recording and connection, not constant brainstorming. Your service solves *content fatigue* with a system that saves hours and helps them show up confidently on mic.

You're also helping them stay consistent and professional, which builds their audience and authority.

Where to Sell or Offer It

- **Fiverr & Upwork**: List as "Podcast Episode Planner" or "AI-Powered Podcast Idea Generator"
- **Instagram or LinkedIn**: DM podcasters with a free preview or offer a first-episode plan free
- **Facebook Groups**: Podcast support communities are filled with your ideal buyers
- **Gumroad or Etsy**: Sell downloadable planners and topic packs
- **Your Website**: Turn this into a subscription or booking-based service

What You'll Need

- ChatGPT to generate episode ideas, outlines, and descriptions
- Google Docs, Notion, or Canva for formatting and delivery
- A simple intake form to gather your client's niche, tone, and content goal
- Optional: Grammarly or Hemingway to polish copy for descriptions or scripts

How Much You Can Charge

- **Episode Idea Packs (20–50 ideas)**: \$50–\$100
- **Monthly Content Plan**: \$100–\$300/month
- **Full Planner Package (ideas + outlines + show notes)**: \$200–\$500
- **Upsells**: Scriptwriting, guest research, title optimization, etc.

Even just 3 clients on a \$250/month plan = \$750/month, recurring. You could also easily sell 100 downloads of a \$29 planner = \$2,900/month.

Tips to Stand Out

- Niche your services: "Podcast Plans for Christian Coaches," "Show Topics for Financial Educators," "Episode Ideas for Relationship Podcasts"
- Offer a 10-topic freebie in exchange for emails
- Bundle this with your **lead magnet (#26)** or **scriptwriting service (#24)** to build a content empire
- Share behind-the-scenes looks at how you generate ideas (build trust + curiosity)

33. Sell AI-Created "Done-for-You" Webinar Scripts and Slide Decks

Webinars are still one of the top ways to sell high-ticket coaching, courses, or digital products—but writing a persuasive webinar script and building the slides is overwhelming for most creators. With AI, you can deliver a complete, structured, and engaging webinar script + slide outline in hours instead of weeks—and turn it into a premium digital service.

What You'll Do

You'll offer a service where you use AI to write:

- Full webinar scripts (including intro, teaching, pitch, and close)
- Slide-by-slide outlines with key talking points
- Title options and hooks
- Call-to-action phrases
- Bonus: Email sequences or landing page copy (for upsell)

You'll ask your client for:

- Their niche and product
- Target audience
- Desired transformation or offer
- Tone (casual, professional, faith-based, etc.)

Example prompt:
"Write a 45-minute webinar script for a Christian life coach selling a $497 6-week women's empowerment program. Include storytelling, scripture, and a soft-sell close."
Or:
"Create a 30-slide webinar outline for a productivity expert teaching how to reclaim your time and make more money from home. Include one main takeaway per slide."
You can also build the slides in Canva (optional), or deliver the content as a Google Doc for the client to plug in.

Why It Works

A great webinar can make thousands of dollars—but most creators struggle with structure, flow, and how to pitch without sounding pushy. You're solving that problem with a done-for-you solution that saves time, removes doubt, and gives them confidence.

Webinar scripting is high-ticket because it directly ties to sales. And since AI does 70% of the writing, your profit margins are big.

Where to Sell or Promote

- **Fiverr & Upwork**: List as “Webinar Scriptwriting + Slide Design”
- **Coaching Facebook Groups**: Creators and coaches often ask for help with their webinars
- **Email List or Instagram**: Offer a free “Webinar Structure Cheat Sheet” to build trust and pitch your service
- **LinkedIn**: Connect with course creators and consultants launching digital offers
- **Your Website**: Position this as a premium service or productized offer

What You’ll Need

- ChatGPT for scriptwriting and outlining
- Google Docs or Notion to deliver the script
- Canva or PowerPoint to create slides (optional)
- Optional: ConvertKit or Flodesk knowledge if offering follow-up emails

How Much You Can Charge

- **Basic Script Only**: $150–$300
- **Script + Slides**: $400–$750
- **Full Webinar Launch Kit**: $1,000+ (includes emails, landing page copy, replay script, etc.)
- **Passive Income Option**: Sell generic webinar scripts + slide templates for $47–$97 each

Two clients per month at $500 = $1,000/month. Five digital sales of a $97 script bundle per week = another $1,940/month.

Tips to Stand Out

- Offer themed versions: “Faith-Based Webinar Template,” “High-Ticket Coaching Sales Webinar,” “Webinar for Digital Product Launches”
- Include bonus slide prompts or Canva templates
- Share testimonials from past clients who converted from your scripts
- Offer a free webinar script framework as a lead magnet

34. Create AI-Written Resume and Cover Letter Templates for Specific Careers

Everyone needs a resume—but most people either don't know how to write one or end up with a generic, boring version that doesn't stand out. With AI, you can create profession-specific resume and cover letter templates that job seekers can customize and use—giving you a simple way to earn from digital products or services with little to no startup cost.

What You'll Do

You'll use AI to:

- Write resumes tailored to specific industries or job titles
- Generate matching cover letters with personalization options
- Create editable templates in Google Docs, Microsoft Word, or Canva
- Add bonus elements like follow-up email templates or reference sheets

You can niche down to careers like:

- Entry-level healthcare workers
- Christian educators
- Remote customer service reps
- Real estate assistants
- Faith-based nonprofit applicants

Example prompt:

"Write a resume for an entry-level Christian school teacher. Include a faith-based summary, classroom management experience, and mission statement."

Or:

"Create a professional but warm cover letter for someone applying to a Christian counseling organization."

You then clean it up, format it nicely, and package it as either:

- A downloadable template
- A custom service
- A kit (resume + cover letter + bonus docs)

Why It Works

People hate writing resumes—and they're willing to pay for ones that are tailored to their industry, values, or desired role. You're offering an easy-to-use product that makes a real difference in someone's job hunt.

Plus, with AI, you can create dozens of versions in different tones and career types in a single day. This makes it perfect for passive income or bulk custom services.

Where to Sell or Promote

- **Etsy**: Great for resume templates in specific niches
- **Gumroad or Payhip**: Sell digital bundles
- **Fiverr & Upwork**: Offer custom resume writing services
- **Facebook Groups**: Job-seeking and career change groups are full of potential buyers
- **Your Website**: Add a digital resume shop or job prep blog

What You'll Need

- ChatGPT for generating resumes and letters
- Google Docs, Word, or Canva for formatting and customization
- Gumroad, Etsy, or your own site for selling
- Optional: Notion if you want to create interactive resume-building dashboards

How Much You Can Charge

- **Digital Templates**: $7–$29
- **Template Bundles**: $30–$75 (includes resume, cover letter, references, follow-up emails)
- **Custom Resume Service**: $100–$300+
- **Upsells**: LinkedIn optimization (#22), interview prep checklist, or job tracker

Sell 100 templates at $19 = $1,900. Or offer 5 custom resumes a month at $200 = $1,000/month in active service income.

Tips to Stand Out

- Niche your templates: "Faith-Based Resume Template," "Remote Job Resume Kit," or "Resume for Christian College Grads"
- Include a "how to use this template" guide or short video
- Offer bonus items like prayer declarations for job seekers, or resume checklists
- Add editable versions for Canva users who want quick design upgrades

35. Build and Sell AI-Generated Niche eNewsletter Templates

Email newsletters are one of the most effective tools for growing and monetizing an audience—but writing them consistently? That's where most people fall off. With AI, you can create **done-for-you newsletter templates** in different niches and either sell them as plug-and-play downloads or offer them as a writing service for creators, coaches, and small business owners.

What You'll Do

You'll use AI to generate:

- Newsletter topics and content sections
- Headlines and subject lines
- Weekly or monthly themes
- Opening hooks and CTAs (calls to action)
- Ready-to-send emails tailored to your client's tone and audience

Popular niches:

- Christian encouragement newsletters
- Wellness tips for moms
- Financial wisdom for beginners
- Motivational emails for entrepreneurs
- Marketing tips for small business owners

Example prompt:

"Create a 4-week Christian inspirational email newsletter with short teachings, scripture references, and a prayer for each week. Each email should be under 300 words."

"Write a weekly email newsletter series for an Etsy seller coach helping creatives grow their shop. Include a helpful tip, a motivational quote, and a product promo section."

You can deliver these as:

- Editable templates (Google Docs, Notion, or Canva)
- Full email sets (written + formatted)
- Subscription content packs (monthly or quarterly)

Why It Works

Newsletters keep audiences warm—but writing them weekly becomes a chore for most creators. Your product or service takes the pressure off and provides a structure that clients can use forever.
Because email = money (especially in digital business), many are willing to pay for pro-level content that boosts engagement and sales. This is also perfect for turning into a **subscription model** or **bundle business**.

Where to Sell or Promote

- **Gumroad, Payhip, or Etsy**: Sell templates and planners
- **Instagram or TikTok**: Show newsletter sneak peeks and writing tips
- **Facebook Groups**: Coaches and creators are often looking for newsletter help
- **Fiverr & Upwork**: Offer newsletter creation gigs
- **Your Website or Email List**: Upsell from a free content planner or lead magnet

What You'll Need

- ChatGPT for idea generation and copywriting
- Google Docs, Canva, or Notion to format templates
- Optional: Email platform access (like ConvertKit or MailerLite) if you're offering to load emails for clients
- Optional: Airtable or Trello if you want to build a "newsletter planning hub"

How Much You Can Charge

- **Basic Template Pack (4–6 emails)**: $29–$49
- **Premium Newsletter Bundle (12+ emails + content calendar)**: $75–$150
- **Custom Newsletter Writing Service**: $200–$500/month per client
- **Subscription Model**: $19–$49/month for new newsletter drops every 30 days

Three clients on a $300 retainer = $900/month recurring. Selling 100 digital packs at $29 = $2,900.

Tips to Stand Out

- Theme your content: "Faith-Based Email Templates for Coaches," "Done-for-You Email Packs for Financial Educators," "Weekly Devotionals for Christian Brands"
- Include subject lines, emojis, and mobile-friendly formatting
- Offer bonuses like Canva headers or call-to-action buttons
- Give away a free 3-email starter kit to grow your list and warm up leads

36. Offer AI-Powered Product Description Writing for Online Stores

eCommerce sellers need strong product descriptions to increase conversions, improve SEO, and stand out—but writing hundreds of them can be exhausting. With AI, you can offer a done-for-you service or digital product that provides **compelling, keyword-rich, and customer-focused product descriptions** for online stores on platforms like Shopify, Etsy, or Amazon.

What You'll Do

You'll use AI to generate:

- Optimized product descriptions (short & long form)
- Feature/benefit breakdowns
- Bullet point highlights
- SEO keyword integration
- Taglines and promotional blurbs

Example prompt:

"Write a persuasive product description for a handmade lavender soy candle. Include benefits, sensory language, and keywords like 'relaxation' and 'stress relief.'"

Or:

"Create a product description for a Christian-themed planner with scriptures, journaling prompts, and habit trackers. Include spiritual encouragement and lifestyle benefits."

You can format these for delivery in:

- Google Docs
- CSV files for mass uploads (great for Etsy or Shopify)
- Templates for ongoing use

Why It Works

Most product listings are either too short, too vague, or keyword-stuffed without emotion. Your AI-assisted service helps sellers write descriptions that *connect* with buyers and convert browsers into customers.

eCommerce sellers value speed and clarity—you'll give them both, saving time and helping boost their store's performance.

Where to Sell or Promote

- **Fiverr & Upwork**: Product listing gigs are in high demand
- **Facebook Groups**: eCommerce and Etsy seller communities
- **Shopify Forums or Reddit**: Offer optimized description packs
- **Email Outreach**: Contact stores with under-optimized listings and offer a sample
- **Your Website**: Offer as a service or downloadable bundle

What You'll Need

- ChatGPT to generate descriptions quickly
- Optional: Google Sheets if delivering bulk descriptions
- Optional: Keyword research tools (Ubersuggest, Keywords Everywhere) for SEO optimization

How Much You Can Charge

- **Single Product Description**: $15–$30
- **Bundles (10–20 products)**: $150–$400
- **Ongoing Monthly Service**: $300–$800/month for shops with rotating inventory
- **Downloadable Templates or DIY Kits**: $19–$49

Write for 5 clients a month at $250 = $1,250/month. Or sell 100 template kits at $29 = $2,900 in digital income.

Tips to Stand Out

- Offer niches: "Descriptions for Handmade Products," "Faith-Based Product Copy," or "Wellness Brands SEO Copy"
- Include before/after examples to show the impact of strong copy
- Add title/headline optimization or upsell email promo blurbs
- Bundle with lead magnet ideas, email marketing copy, or website about-page upgrades

37. Offer AI-Powered Course Quiz & Test Creation for Educators and Coaches

Coaches, online teachers, and course creators often need quizzes, assessments, or knowledge checks to keep their students engaged—but writing those questions takes time. With AI, you can create **custom quizzes, tests, and reflection questions** for digital courses, workbooks, or live trainings—and sell this as a valuable add-on service.

What You'll Do

You'll use AI to generate:

- Multiple choice quizzes
- Short answer questions
- Knowledge checks by module
- True/false tests
- Reflection and discussion questions
- Answer keys or explanations

Example AI prompts:

"Create a 10-question quiz for Module 2 of a course on Christian entrepreneurship. Include multiple choice, true/false, and 2 reflection questions."

"Write a final test for a 4-week course on overcoming limiting beliefs. Include 15 questions with answers and scoring suggestions."

You'll organize the quizzes into:

- PDF or Word documents
- Google Forms (for clients to plug into)
- LMS-ready formats for platforms like Teachable, Thinkific, or Kajabi

Why It Works

Course creators want to measure progress—but writing quality quizzes is a time-consuming task most skip. When you offer AI-assisted quiz creation, you save them hours, make their course more professional, and increase student engagement and retention.

Educators, homeschoolers, and even faith-based program leaders also need testing content but often lack the structure or creativity to build it themselves.

Where to Sell or Offer It

- **Fiverr & Upwork**: Create a gig like "Course Quiz Creation for Online Teachers & Coaches"
- **Facebook Groups**: Course creator or digital product groups
- **Instagram & LinkedIn**: DM coaches or consultants launching new programs
- **Your Website**: Add as a service next to your writing or curriculum offers
- **Bundle with Course Outline Services**: Like idea #16

What You'll Need

- ChatGPT to create the quizzes and answer keys
- Google Docs or Canva to format the documents
- Google Forms or Typeform (optional for delivery)
- Optional: Knowledge of LMS platforms if you want to help upload

How Much You Can Charge

- **Basic Quiz Pack (1 module)**: $50–$100
- **Full Course Quiz Pack**: $200–$500
- **Ongoing Content Creation**: $300+/month for ongoing support or multi-course creators
- **Digital Templates**: $29–$59 for downloadable DIY quiz builders

Just 4 clients at $250 = $1,000/month. Or sell 50 quiz templates at $39 = $1,950.

Tips to Stand Out

- Niche by subject: "Quizzes for Christian Coaching Programs," "Assessments for Homeschooling Moms," "Tests for Business Courses"
- Include bonus questions like journaling prompts or scriptural reflection (for faith-based creators)
- Offer scoring rubrics and certificates of completion
- Bundle with your course scriptwriting (#16) or lead magnet services (#26)

38. Offer AI-Created Job Interview Preparation Kits

Job seekers often feel overwhelmed preparing for interviews—especially when it comes to anticipating questions, crafting strong answers, and building confidence. With AI, you can provide personalized **Job Interview Prep Kits** that simulate real questions, help candidates prepare compelling responses, and offer confidence-boosting strategies—all based on their role, industry, or background.

What You'll Do

You'll use AI to create:

- Mock interview questions (customized by job title and company)
- Suggested answers or talking points
- Strengths/weaknesses templates
- STAR method responses (Situation, Task, Action, Result)
- Industry-specific do's and don'ts
- Bonus: Mindset prep tips and prayer or affirmation guides (for faith-based clients)

Example prompts:

"Generate 10 behavioral interview questions for a faith-based nonprofit leadership position, with example answers based on biblical principles."

"Write a personalized interview prep guide for someone applying to a tech startup as a project manager. Include common questions, STAR method sample answers, and 5 confidence tips."

You can format these into:

- Printable PDFs
- Editable Google Docs
- Personalized bundles sent via email
- Plug-and-play Notion dashboards or Trello boards

Why It Works

People fear interviews more than resumes. You're not just giving them information—you're preparing them emotionally and mentally to *show up well*. It's a high-value, low-overhead offer, and it works in *any industry*.

Plus, job seekers often spend money on resume services or coaching. This fits naturally into that buying behavior and helps you stand out with a *tangible, confidence-focused tool.*

Where to Sell or Promote

- **Fiverr & Upwork**: Offer "Custom Job Interview Prep Kit" as a premium gig
- **Career Facebook Groups**: Target job seekers, grads, or returning professionals
- **Christian Communities**: Provide spiritual-centered interview kits with prayer support
- **LinkedIn or IG**: DM job seekers or new grads offering a free preview
- **Your Website**: Bundle this with resume services (#1) or LinkedIn optimization (#22)

What You'll Need

- ChatGPT to generate questions and response examples
- Google Docs or Canva for formatting
- Optional: Trello or Notion templates for a more interactive delivery
- Optional: Your own list of best interview questions by niche or industry

How Much You Can Charge

- **Basic Kit**: $50–$100 (includes 10 questions and sample answers)
- **Deluxe Kit**: $150–$300 (includes questions, STAR answers, mindset tips, and bonus material)
- **Subscription Model**: $29/month for access to a growing library of prep kits by industry
- **Upsell**: Live mock interview session for an extra $100+

Even just 5 clients/month at $150 = $750. Pair this with resume services and you can offer full packages easily worth $500+.

Tips to Stand Out

- Include a "faith-centered confidence boost" for Christian audiences (prayer, verses, affirmations)
- Offer kits by profession: "Teacher Interview Prep Kit," "Tech Startup Job Kit," "Faith-Based Career Prep"
- Bundle this with application trackers, follow-up email templates, or thank-you note scripts
- Record a short video walking the buyer through their prep guide—adds huge value!

39. Offer AI-Powered Brand Voice and Messaging Guides

Most business owners know what they *do*, but they struggle to communicate *how they sound*—consistently. With AI, you can create **custom Brand Voice and Messaging Guides** that help entrepreneurs, content creators, and small businesses clearly define their tone, vocabulary, personality, and key phrases—so they show up with confidence in every piece of content.

What You'll Do

You'll use AI to generate:

- Brand tone descriptions (e.g., "warm but bold," "faith-filled but professional")
- Example phrases, taglines, and slogans
- "Do say / Don't say" lists
- Sample social media captions or bios
- Elevator pitch and about-me copy
- Messaging pillars (3–5 core themes they should always communicate)

Example prompt:
"Create a brand voice guide for a Christian women's coach who helps burned-out moms rediscover purpose. Include tone, keywords, tagline ideas, and example phrases."
Or:
"Write a messaging guide for a Gen Z fitness influencer who wants to sound funny, bold, and relatable on Instagram."
You'll organize everything into a clean, branded PDF or Google Doc that your client can use across their website, social media, emails, and videos.

Why It Works

Most people sound inconsistent online because they don't have a defined voice. But *brand consistency builds trust*—and trust leads to conversions.
Your AI-assisted guide gives entrepreneurs a major confidence boost and sets them up for professional communication across platforms.
This service also positions you as a high-value creative strategist, not "just a writer."

Where to Sell or Promote

- **Fiverr & Upwork**: Offer "Brand Voice Style Guide" or "Messaging Strategy Document"
- **Facebook Groups for Coaches & Creators**: These buyers often don't know they need this until they see it!
- **Instagram or TikTok**: Share brand tone makeovers or "before and after" bios
- **Your Website**: Offer as a package or upsell to copywriting or content planning clients

What You'll Need

- ChatGPT to generate descriptions, examples, and copy
- Canva, Notion, or Google Docs for layout
- Optional: Grammarly for polishing
- Optional: A simple intake form to learn about your client's personality and audience

How Much You Can Charge

- **Basic Brand Voice Guide**: $100–$200
- **Complete Messaging Pack (bio, pitch, captions)**: $300–$600
- **Course Creator or Coach Bundle**: $750+ including voice + content strategy
- **Downloadable Templates**: $39–$59 for DIYers

Just 4 clients/month at $250 = $1,000. Or 100 template sales at $39 = $3,900 in passive income.

Tips to Stand Out

- Niche your guides: "Faith-Based Coaches," "Wellness Creators," "Bold Black Women Entrepreneurs"
- Include a brand tone test (multiple choice) to help people self-identify their voice
- Offer a sample page as a free lead magnet: "Define Your Brand Voice in 10 Minutes"
- Bundle with your bios (#28), LinkedIn optimization (#22), or email templates (#35)

40. Use AI to Create and Sell Digital Planners for Niche Lifestyles

Planners are everywhere—but the real money is in **niche digital planners** that speak directly to someone's lifestyle, values, or goals. With AI, you can create ultra-specific digital planners filled with prompts, trackers, and layouts for your audience—and sell them as downloadable PDFs or interactive digital tools.

What You'll Do

You'll use AI to generate:

- Daily, weekly, or monthly planning prompts
- Guided reflection or journaling questions
- Productivity, habit, and prayer trackers
- Meal planning, budgeting, fitness, or goal-setting sections
- Niche-specific encouragements or scriptures

Example prompts:

"Create a 30-day digital planner for Christian moms managing homeschooling, household chores, and personal spiritual time. Include prayer prompts, meal planning space, and scripture reflection sections."

"Write content for a monthly digital business planner for Gen Z entrepreneurs. Include goal-setting templates, social media planning, and weekly check-ins."

Once the content is generated, you'll use **Canva** or similar tools to design:

- Printable planner pages
- Fillable PDFs
- Hyperlinked digital planners for iPad/GoodNotes

Why It Works

Generic planners are boring. But when someone sees a planner designed *just for them*—their lifestyle, beliefs, or challenges—they buy it. And because planners are mostly copy + layout, you can create dozens of them with minimal cost using AI and free design tools. Plus, planners are **evergreen**—people use them year-round and often repurchase every quarter or season.

Where to Sell or Promote

- **Etsy**: A top platform for faith-based and lifestyle planner sales
- **Gumroad or Payhip**: Sell bundles, upsells, or multi-format planners
- **Instagram or TikTok**: Create reels showing what's inside each planner
- **Pinterest**: Use visuals to drive traffic to your store
- **Your Website**: Build a brand around productivity or digital planning

What You'll Need

- ChatGPT to write planner content and prompts
- Canva to design printable and digital layouts
- Gumroad, Etsy, or your site to sell
- Optional: Use PDF Escape, Adobe, or Keynote to make fillable or hyperlinked versions

How Much You Can Charge

- **Basic Printable Planner**: \$10–\$19
- **Hyperlinked Digital Planner**: \$25–\$45
- **Niche Bundles (3+ planners)**: \$49–\$99
- **Custom Planner Service**: \$150–\$300+ for personal branding or business clients

Sell 100 planners at \$19 = \$1,900. Create 5 niche planners and sell them monthly = passive income flow.

Tips to Stand Out

- Go ultra-niche: "Faith & Fitness Planner for Busy Women," "Content Planner for Christian Creators," "Healing After Divorce Planner"
- Include digital sticker packs or wallpaper bundles as bonuses
- Offer seasonal or monthly versions (great for returning customers)
- Pair your planner with a **lead magnet** or mini course

41. Launch an AI-Powered Weekly Niche Newsletter as a Paid Subscription

Email newsletters are no longer just for updates—they're full-blown content businesses. With AI, you can create a **paid weekly newsletter** tailored to a specific niche, delivering curated insights, original writing, and resources your audience looks forward to every week—all without needing to write from scratch.

What You'll Do

You'll use AI to:

- Generate newsletter content based on niche topics
- Curate industry trends, quotes, tips, or scripture
- Create headlines, hooks, and CTAs
- Summarize articles or videos
- Add a personal intro or spiritual reflection (edited or written by you)

Niche examples:

- Christian entrepreneurship insights
- Weekly devotionals + mindset shifts
- Financial wisdom for Millennials
- Content strategy for coaches
- AI tools for small business owners

Example prompt:

"Write a weekly email for a paid newsletter called 'Faith to Build.' Include a biblical reflection, 1 business tip for Christian entrepreneurs, and a recommended tool or scripture of the week."

"Create a 4-week paid newsletter series for freelance designers. Each email should include a creative business tip, a motivational quote, and a mini client challenge."

You can start with 4–8 emails scheduled ahead, use AI to build each issue, and personalize it as needed.

Why It Works

People want focused content from someone they trust—and they're willing to pay $5–$15/month for insights, encouragement, or shortcuts that save time or fuel their purpose. A paid newsletter is low-cost to run, high-leverage for income, and perfect for building authority in your space.

Once built, it becomes a scalable digital asset that grows month after month.

Where to Sell or Promote

- **Substack**: Perfect for paid newsletter launches and growing a following
- **ConvertKit or MailerLite**: Great for automating and growing your own list
- **Instagram Reels or TikTok**: Share highlights from each issue
- **Gumroad**: Offer access to back issues or bundle yearly subscriptions
- **Your Website**: Sell as a subscription offer or bonus with coaching/digital products

What You'll Need

- ChatGPT for writing and structuring newsletter issues
- Substack, ConvertKit, or MailerLite for delivery
- Stripe or Gumroad to process payments (if not using Substack)
- Optional: Canva for creating header images or embedded visuals

How Much You Can Charge

- **Monthly Subscription**: $5–$15/month
- **Annual Plan**: $49–$99/year
- **Premium Tier**: $20–$49/month (include templates, community access, or coaching clips)
- **Add-On**: Sell old issues or archive access for a one-time price

100 subscribers at $9/month = $900/month recurring. With consistent promotion, this can scale to 500+ easily.

Tips to Stand Out

- Be niche and consistent: "The Bold Christian Boss," "The Freelance Fix," "Money & Mindset Monday"
- Include weekly segments: Quote of the week, scripture, challenge, resource
- Offer a free version with previews or excerpts to grow your list
- Pair this with your **affirmation kits, planners, or templates** for more value

42. Create AI-Generated Sermon or Bible Study Outlines for Ministries and Leaders

Pastors, youth leaders, and small group teachers often struggle with time when it comes to preparing weekly sermons or Bible study materials. With AI, you can offer **customized sermon outlines, small group studies, and teaching notes** that help them stay inspired, organized, and on message—all while saving them hours every week.

What You'll Do

You'll use AI to:

- Generate sermon outlines based on themes or scriptures
- Create small group discussion guides
- Write reflection questions and prayer prompts
- Suggest opening hooks, illustrations, and scriptures
- Format study guides for teaching, digital delivery, or printouts

Example prompts:

"Write a 3-point sermon outline for youth ministry on the topic of 'Overcoming Fear.' Include scripture references, application points, and a short closing prayer."

"Create a 4-week Bible study for women on the theme of 'Purpose and Identity in Christ.' Each session should include a main scripture, teaching notes, and 5 discussion questions."

You can deliver your content as:

- Editable PDFs or Word Docs
- PowerPoint slides or Canva templates
- Downloadable packs or bundles (for specific audiences or seasons)
- Custom monthly service for churches or ministries

Why It Works

Ministry leaders are often juggling multiple roles—preaching, leading, mentoring, admin—and content prep can be overwhelming. Your outlines don't replace their voice—they *support* it by giving structure, inspiration, and clarity.

And because spiritual content is evergreen and always in demand, this can become a powerful recurring or passive income stream.

Where to Sell or Promote

- **Facebook Groups**: Target pastors, women's ministries, youth leaders
- **Your Website**: Build a "Resources for Leaders" section or membership
- **Etsy**: Yes—faith-based digital downloads do well there
- **Gumroad**: Sell sermon packs, series, or seasonal outlines
- **Email List**: Build a list of ministry leaders and deliver fresh resources monthly

What You'll Need

- ChatGPT to generate outlines, scriptures, and teaching points
- Canva for design (covers, slides, or workbook format)
- Google Docs or PDFs for easy sharing
- Optional: Create a membership area for recurring access to new content

How Much You Can Charge

- **Single Sermon or Study Outline**: $10–$25
- **Series Pack (4–6 weeks)**: $50–$100
- **Monthly Subscription**: $20–$49/month for fresh outlines & studies
- **Custom Writing Service**: $150–$300/month for pastors or churches

Sell 50 series packs at $50 = $2,500. Or 40 subscribers at $29/month = $1,160/month recurring.

Tips to Stand Out

- Niche your offerings: "Sermons for Youth," "Small Group for Christian Entrepreneurs," "Women's Bible Study Series"
- Include reflection or journaling pages with each study
- Offer seasonal packs: "Advent Series," "New Year in Christ," "Resurrection Power"
- Bundle with your other faith-based products (like devotionals or planners)

43. Use AI to Create and Sell Email Autoresponder Sequences for Digital Product Sellers

Selling digital products online? That first sale is just the beginning. Smart creators know the money is in the **follow-up**. With AI, you can offer **automated email sequences** (a.k.a. autoresponders) that help sellers nurture leads, build trust, and sell more of their products—without having to manually write each email.

What You'll Do

You'll use AI to generate:

- Welcome sequences (3–7 emails after someone signs up)
- Product launch email series
- Abandoned cart follow-ups
- Upsell and cross-sell sequences
- Seasonal or holiday promo sequences
- Re-engagement emails for "cold" subscribers

Example prompt:

"Write a 5-email welcome series for a Christian Etsy seller who sells printable devotionals. Emails should include encouragement, product tips, and soft calls to buy more."

"Create a 7-email launch sequence for a digital course on productivity for new entrepreneurs. Use an inspiring but direct tone with urgency built in."

You'll customize these sequences and format them for easy upload into tools like ConvertKit, MailerLite, or Flodesk.

Why It Works

Digital product sellers are great at creating—but not always great at selling. Email marketing helps them turn *one-time buyers* into *lifelong customers*—but writing strategic sequences takes time and skill. You're offering them a shortcut to increased income, better brand connection, and long-term results.

Where to Sell or Offer It

- **Fiverr & Upwork**: Offer "Email Sequence for Etsy Sellers," "Course Launch Emails," etc.
- **Instagram or TikTok**: Post before/after email copy examples

- **Facebook Groups**: Target sellers in Etsy, Gumroad, Kajabi, or digital marketing groups
- **Your Website**: Bundle as a service or offer as downloadable plug-and-play sequences
- **Email Marketers & VAs**: Partner with them to offer copy services to their clients

What You'll Need

- ChatGPT to create the email sequences
- Google Docs for delivery
- Optional: Access to email marketing platforms to help with implementation
- Optional: Grammarly for final polishing

How Much You Can Charge

- **Welcome Series (3–5 emails)**: $100–$250
- **Launch or Promo Series (5–8 emails)**: $200–$500
- **Full Funnel Package (12+ emails)**: $500–$1,000+
- **Template Packs for Sellers**: $39–$79 per niche (passive product)

Sell 5 launch sequences at $300 = $1,500/month. Or create 3 email packs at $49 and sell 100 = $4,900 passive.

Tips to Stand Out

- Niche down: "Sequences for Faith-Based Product Sellers," "Email Funnels for Etsy Coaches," "Launch Emails for Printable Courses"
- Include CTAs and subject line options in every package
- Offer "fill-in-the-blank" templates for DIY users
- Bundle with lead magnet creation (#26) or sales page copywriting

44. Sell AI-Generated FAQs and Knowledge Base Content for Websites

Many small businesses, creators, and digital product sellers struggle to explain everything their audience might ask—especially on websites. With AI, you can create comprehensive, **Frequently Asked Questions (FAQ)** sections or full **Knowledge Base articles** that answer customer concerns, reduce support emails, and boost trust and conversions.

What You'll Do

You'll use AI to:

- Generate FAQ sections based on a product, service, or niche
- Write detailed answers with clear, brand-aligned language
- Create knowledge base articles, tutorials, or how-to guides
- Format responses for websites, PDFs, or customer service portals

Example prompts:

"Write an FAQ section for a Christian business coach offering a 6-week coaching program. Include questions about scheduling, payments, refunds, and what's included."

"Create a knowledge base article explaining how to download and print digital wall art from an Etsy shop. Include troubleshooting tips."

You can deliver content in:

- Google Docs (for copy/paste use)
- PDF handouts (for digital shops)
- CMS-ready format (for platforms like Wix, WordPress, or Shopify)

Why It Works

A clear FAQ or Help section makes people *buy faster and complain less*. It's also one of the most overlooked parts of online businesses. You're not just creating content—you're improving conversions, reducing support workload, and building customer confidence.

This is especially valuable for:

- Etsy or digital shop owners
- Coaches or course creators
- eCommerce businesses
- Churches and ministries with online giving or event registration

Where to Sell or Offer It

- **Fiverr & Upwork**: Create gigs for "Website FAQs," "Knowledge Base Setup," or "Etsy Shop Help Docs"
- **Facebook Groups**: Target digital product sellers, coaches, or Shopify owners
- **Your Website**: Offer this as a premium copywriting service
- **Gumroad or Etsy**: Sell template bundles like "25 FAQ Templates for Etsy Sellers" or "Knowledge Base Guide for Coaches"

What You'll Need

- ChatGPT to generate FAQ content and articles
- Google Docs or Canva to format for delivery
- Optional: Website backend access if you're uploading it for clients
- Optional: Grammarly for polishing tone and grammar

How Much You Can Charge

- **Basic FAQ Section**: $50–$150 (5–10 questions + answers)
- **Knowledge Base Article Pack (3–5 articles)**: $200–$500
- **Full Website FAQ + Knowledge Center Setup**: $500–$1,000+
- **Template Pack for DIY Sellers**: $29–$59 (great for passive income)

Sell 10 FAQ packs at $150 = $1,500. Or offer a monthly knowledge base update service to digital product creators at $250/month.

Tips to Stand Out

- Niche down: "FAQs for Christian Coaching Programs," "Knowledge Base for Etsy Sellers," "Support Docs for Print-on-Demand Shops"
- Offer screenshots or step-by-step visuals (optional Canva design upsell)
- Add customer service email templates or automated responses
- Bundle with your product description service (#36) or email autoresponder offer (#43)

45. Create AI-Generated Social Media Caption Packs for Niche Audiences

Social media content is a daily struggle for many creators, coaches, and business owners. They have the photos or ideas—but not the *words*. With AI, you can create and sell **pre-written caption packs** tailored to specific niches, tones, and platforms, helping others post consistently without writer's block.

What You'll Do

You'll use AI to generate:

- Daily or weekly social media captions
- Content organized by theme (motivation, sales, storytelling, tips)
- Platform-specific styles (Instagram, Facebook, LinkedIn, TikTok hooks)
- Hashtag suggestions and call-to-action lines
- Seasonal content (holiday campaigns, launches, etc.)

Example prompts:

"Create 30 Instagram captions for a Christian business coach targeting faith-based entrepreneurs. Include encouragement, soft-selling, and scripture-based inspiration."

"Write a 2-week LinkedIn caption series for a productivity expert promoting a digital planner. Keep it casual, actionable, and clear."

You can package the captions into:

- Canva-designed content calendars
- Copy/paste Google Docs
- Plug-and-play social media planners
- Editable Notion templates

Why It Works

Content is king—but consistency is queen. Most entrepreneurs know they need to post, but don't know *what to say*. Your caption packs offer ready-made, scroll-stopping copy that saves time, drives engagement, and helps them sell or connect more authentically.

It's high perceived value and easy to reproduce across multiple niches with AI.

Where to Sell or Promote

- **Etsy & Gumroad**: Sell as downloadable packs

- **Fiverr & Upwork**: Offer custom or niche caption writing
- **Instagram & TikTok**: Promote using real caption examples in reels or carousels
- **Facebook Groups**: Coaches, creators, and solopreneurs are always looking for content help
- **Your Website**: Add to a "Content Tools" section with caption bundles and planners

What You'll Need

- ChatGPT for fast, niche-specific caption writing
- Canva or Google Docs for delivery
- Optional: Scheduling tools like Later or Buffer (for upsell support)
- Optional: Trello or Notion templates if offering content planning boards

How Much You Can Charge

- **30-Caption Packs**: $19–$39
- **90-Day Content Calendar with Captions**: $59–$99
- **Custom Caption Writing (per client)**: $150–$400/project
- **Membership Model**: $29–$59/month for fresh monthly packs

Sell 100 caption packs at $29 = $2,900. Add 10 subscribers at $39/month = $390/month recurring.

Tips to Stand Out

- Niche by tone or audience: "Bold Captions for Christian Women," "Soft-Sell Content for Wellness Coaches," "Product Promo Captions for Etsy Shops"
- Offer plug-and-play templates that match reels, carousels, or static posts
- Include content prompts and repurposing ideas
- Bundle with your content calendar service (#31) or email newsletter copy (#35)

46. Offer AI-Generated Video Script Templates for Reels, Shorts, and TikToks

Short-form video is the #1 way to grow a brand online—but most creators struggle with *what to say* in those crucial first 3–7 seconds. With AI, you can create and sell **video script templates** specifically for Reels, YouTube Shorts, and TikToks that help creators hook their audience, deliver value fast, and increase engagement.

What You'll Do

You'll use AI to write:

- Hook-intro-delivery-CTA scripts
- 15–60 second video scripts for specific niches
- Storytelling or testimonial frameworks
- Trend-based remixes or ideas
- Call-to-action closings that drive followers, sign-ups, or sales

Example prompts:

"Write 10 30-second TikTok video scripts for a Christian entrepreneur offering coaching services. Each should start with a scroll-stopping hook and end with a faith-based CTA."

"Create 7 short-form video scripts for a digital product seller promoting Canva templates. Include product mentions and storytelling-style delivery."

You can format your scripts in:

- Google Docs (organized by day or type)
- Canva video script planners
- Editable Notion or Trello boards
- Slide decks with delivery tips and visual direction

Why It Works

Most creators freeze on camera because they don't know *how* to deliver their message quickly. These AI-written scripts give them the structure and confidence to post consistently—and improve video retention and conversions.

And since short-form content is exploding, you can sell script packs by niche or offer custom services to busy creators.

Where to Sell or Promote

- **Fiverr & Upwork**: Offer "Reels/TikTok Scriptwriting" for specific industries

- **Etsy or Gumroad**: Sell ready-made script packs by topic
- **Instagram or TikTok**: Share videos using your own scripts as proof they work
- **Facebook Groups**: Especially where creators, coaches, or influencers hang out
- **Your Website**: Bundle with content calendars, caption packs, or video coaching

What You'll Need

- ChatGPT to write scripts and callouts
- Google Docs, Canva, or Notion for delivery
- Optional: Loom or Canva Video to show sample delivery
- Optional: Social media scheduler to help clients implement (Later, Metricool, etc.)

How Much You Can Charge

- **Script Packs (10–30 scripts)**: $29–$79
- **Custom Script Service**: $150–$300 per project
- **Monthly Subscription**: $39–$99/month for fresh scripts + content prompts
- **Upsell**: Matching captions, hashtags, or editing direction

Sell 100 script packs at $39 = $3,900. Land 4 monthly clients at $59 = $236/month recurring.

Tips to Stand Out

- Focus by niche: "Reels for Faith-Based Coaches," "Shorts for Etsy Sellers," "TikTok Hooks for Online Teachers"
- Include optional trending audio ideas or post timing tips
- Add a "Filming Tips" cheat sheet for beginners
- Bundle with your social caption packs (#45) and content calendar (#31)

47. Build and Sell AI-Generated Conversation Starters or Icebreaker Packs

Whether it's for date nights, youth groups, networking events, coaching calls, or family dinners—everyone loves a good conversation starter. With AI, you can create niche-specific **conversation decks** or **icebreaker packs** that help people connect deeply, laugh together, or reflect—turning it into a simple, low-cost product with massive appeal.

What You'll Do

You'll use AI to generate:

- Fun or deep icebreaker questions
- Relationship conversation starters
- Group discussion prompts
- Family dinner or youth group questions
- Coaching client warm-up questions

You can niche your packs for:

- Christian couples or marriage ministry
- Coaches working with new clients
- Small group leaders and churches
- Business team retreats or mastermind groups
- Parents and teens looking to connect

Example prompts:

"Create 50 deep conversation starters for Christian couples to use on date night. Include questions about faith, dreams, and emotional connection."

"Write 30 icebreaker questions for teens in a youth group that are fun, clean, and engaging."

You can format and deliver as:

- PDF cards (printable or digital)
- Canva-designed decks
- Flashcard-style mobile downloads
- Gamified versions (e.g., "Pick a number and answer this")

Why It Works

People crave connection—but they often don't know how to *start* meaningful conversations. Your product solves that awkward silence with ready-made prompts that spark dialogue and deepen

relationships. They're great for couples, small groups, events, and retreats.
And they're easy to bundle with journals, devotionals, or coaching tools for even more value.

Where to Sell or Promote

- **Etsy**: Great for printable card decks or date night products
- **Gumroad or Payhip**: Sell as digital downloads
- **Instagram Reels or TikTok**: Show 3 questions from your deck to build interest
- **Facebook Groups**: Share themed questions in relevant faith-based or coaching groups
- **Your Website**: Bundle into your resource shop for families, churches, or creators

What You'll Need

- ChatGPT to generate prompts quickly
- Canva to design printable cards or decks
- Gumroad, Etsy, or your own site to sell
- Optional: Google Sheets or Trello format for coaches or facilitators

How Much You Can Charge

- **Small Packs (20–30 questions)**: $5–$15
- **Full Decks (50–100+ questions)**: $19–$39
- **Custom Packs (with branding)**: $100–$300 for coaches, churches, or therapists
- **Bundle Offers**: $49–$99 (deck + journal + guidebook)

Sell 200 card decks at $15 = $3,000. Offer 5 custom branded packs to coaches at $200 = $1,000.

Tips to Stand Out

- Focus on connection-based themes: "Faith-Filled Questions for Couples," "Deep Talk for Teens," "Break the Ice for Virtual Teams"
- Include fun categories or themes (e.g., "Spicy or Spiritual?")
- Offer blank templates for people to write their own questions
- Bundle with your **journals (#37)**, **workbooks**, or **devotionals**

48. Create AI-Written Digital Welcome Kits for Online Communities and Memberships

When someone joins an online membership, coaching program, or private group, their first experience sets the tone. With AI, you can craft **digital welcome kits** that help creators and community leaders onboard new members with professionalism, clarity, and warmth—without spending hours writing everything from scratch.

What You'll Do

You'll use AI to generate:

- Personalized welcome letters or emails
- Community guidelines and expectations
- Access instructions and FAQs
- Introduce-yourself post templates
- Tips to get the most out of the group or program
- Bonus: Prayer, scripture, or motivational messages (if faith-based)

Example prompts:

"Write a warm and friendly welcome email for new members joining a Christian women's mastermind group. Include a short devotional, a summary of what to expect, and links to onboarding resources."

"Create a full digital welcome kit for a membership community for digital product creators. Include a greeting, access guide, community rules, and FAQs."

You'll package the content as:

- Editable PDFs or Canva kits
- Word Docs for email sequences
- Slide decks for onboarding walkthroughs
- Downloadable packs delivered after sign-up

Why It Works

A smooth onboarding process keeps members engaged, reduces confusion, and boosts retention. But most creators don't have time to build one from scratch. You're offering a shortcut that instantly upgrades their brand and improves customer experience.

These kits also reduce support requests and make the community feel more valuable from day one.

Where to Sell or Offer It

- **Fiverr & Upwork**: "Welcome Kit for Membership or Online Group"
- **Facebook Groups**: Pitch to group admins or new course creators
- **Your Website**: Add to your list of digital services or digital product shop
- **Email Marketing Creators**: Partner with them to offer onboarding content for their clients
- **Gumroad or Etsy**: Sell editable kits as templates by niche

What You'll Need

- ChatGPT to write the welcome content and emails
- Canva or Google Docs to format
- Optional: Access to the community (for customization if doing high-end services)
- Optional: ConvertKit, MailerLite, or Flodesk knowledge for automated delivery

How Much You Can Charge

- **Basic Welcome Kit (PDF)**: $50–$150
- **Premium Branded Kit (email series + guidebook)**: $250–$500
- **Custom Setup + Automation Support**: $500–$1,000+
- **Digital Template Packs**: $29–$59 (passive product)

Sell 50 templates at $39 = $1,950. Or land 4 clients/month at $300 = $1,200 monthly.

Tips to Stand Out

- Niche your kits: "Welcome Kit for Faith-Based Communities," "Coaching Group Onboarding Pack," "Membership Site Starter Kit"
- Include spiritual encouragement or scriptures for Christian audiences
- Offer versions for paid and free groups
- Bundle with email autoresponder setups (#43) or community management tools

49. Sell AI-Generated Podcast Show Notes and Time-Stamped Summaries

Podcasters love recording—but they *hate* writing show notes. With AI, you can provide **professional podcast show notes**, summaries, timestamps, and even SEO-optimized descriptions that help podcasters grow their audience, repurpose content, and look more polished across platforms.

What You'll Do

You'll use AI (plus a transcript or audio input) to:

- Write short and long show descriptions
- Pull out main talking points
- Add time-stamped topic breakdowns
- Generate SEO-friendly titles and tags
- Highlight guest bios and resources mentioned

Example prompt:
"Create show notes and timestamps for a 40-minute Christian entrepreneurship podcast featuring a guest who talks about trusting God during a business pivot."
"Write SEO-optimized show notes for a podcast episode about productivity habits. Include a 3-sentence summary, timestamps for each main point, and a call-to-action."
Once AI generates the content, you'll polish it and deliver it in:

- Google Docs or Notion pages
- Canva templates for blog/social sharing
- WordPress-ready formatting for episode posts

Why It Works

Great show notes improve discoverability, make your podcast easier to repurpose into social content, and help listeners jump to the parts they care about. Most podcasters skip this step—or do it poorly. You're offering a time-saving, high-perceived-value service they *really need.* You're also helping them look more professional to sponsors, guests, and new listeners.

Where to Sell or Offer It

- **Fiverr & Upwork**: "Podcast Show Notes Writer with Timestamps and SEO"

- **Podcast Facebook Groups**: Pitch your service or offer a free trial episode
- **Instagram or LinkedIn**: Share carousel posts with before/after show note examples
- **Your Website**: Add a "Podcast Services" tab with a monthly package
- **Email Lists**: Target podcasters and offer bundled editing + notes packages

What You'll Need

- ChatGPT or other AI tools for summarizing and formatting
- Descript or Otter.ai to transcribe audio
- Google Docs or Notion to organize notes
- Optional: SEO tools like Ubersuggest for title optimization

How Much You Can Charge

- **Per Episode (Basic)**: $40–$100
- **Premium (with timestamps + SEO + links)**: $100–$200
- **Monthly Package (4–8 episodes)**: $300–$800
- **Template Pack**: $25–$49 (for DIY podcasters)

Just 4 clients at $400/month = $1,600 recurring. Add 100 template downloads at $29 = $2,900 passive.

Tips to Stand Out

- Focus on niches: "Show Notes for Faith-Based Podcasts," "Business Coaches," or "Therapists Who Podcast"
- Offer 1 free episode as a sample
- Add title optimization and CTA suggestions to boost engagement
- Bundle with video shorts, blog repurposing, or quote card design

50. Use AI to Create and Sell Bible-Themed Coloring Books

Coloring books aren't just for kids anymore. With AI, you can create **Bible-based coloring books** for children, teens, or adults, combining scriptures, devotionals, and beautiful line art that promote both creativity and spiritual reflection. These make perfect printables, gifts, or physical books on platforms like Etsy and Amazon.

What You'll Do

You'll use AI to:

- Select scriptures based on themes (peace, strength, healing, purpose)
- Write short devotionals or reflections to match each verse
- Create prompts or prayers to pair with coloring pages
- Use AI image tools (like DALL·E or Midjourney) to generate line-art illustrations

Popular themes:

- Bible verses for kids
- Faith-based affirmations for women
- Scriptures about anxiety, hope, or purpose
- Coloring devotionals for families or couples

Example prompts:

"Create 20 encouraging Bible verses with short devotionals for a Christian coloring book titled 'Peace in His Presence.' Each should include a calming scripture and a 2-sentence reflection."

"Generate kid-friendly memory verses and matching themes for a coloring book for children ages 4–8. Include a line about what the verse means."

Why It Works

Christian families, homeschoolers, and ministries are always looking for wholesome, spiritually encouraging resources. A faith-based coloring book becomes a powerful tool for relaxation, learning, and worship—and since it's evergreen, it sells year-round.

You can also create themed versions for holidays, women's retreats, small groups, or youth ministry programs.

Where to Sell or Promote

- **Etsy**: Ideal for printable versions
- **Amazon KDP**: Sell as a physical book or Kindle version
- **Gumroad or Payhip**: Offer PDF downloads
- **Christian Facebook Groups**: Parents, teachers, and leaders are active buyers
- **Instagram & Pinterest**: Share sample pages and quotes to drive traffic

What You'll Need

- ChatGPT to write scriptures, devotionals, and reflection prompts
- Canva or Book Bolt for formatting
- AI image generator (DALL·E, Midjourney) for clean, royalty-free line art
- Amazon KDP or Etsy shop for distribution

How Much You Can Charge

- **Printable Coloring Book (15–30 pages)**: $9–$19
- **Physical Book via Amazon KDP**: $10.99–$14.99
- **Bundles**: $25–$39 for themed sets (e.g., 3 books or seasonal packs)
- **Custom Ministry Versions**: $100–$300+ (branded for churches, events, etc.)

Sell 100 digital books at $12 = $1,200. Or create one Amazon bestseller with consistent sales and royalty checks every month.

Tips to Stand Out

- Niche deep: "Bible Verses for Anxiety," "Scripture Coloring for Girls," "Couples' Devotional Coloring Book"
- Offer bonus items like bookmarks, scripture cards, or prayer journal pages
- Add short prayers or action challenges under each coloring page
- Bundle with devotionals, journals, or activity books for extra value

51. Offer AI-Powered Book Title and Subtitle Brainstorming Services for Authors

Authors often struggle to find the *perfect* title that grabs attention, sells the vision, and speaks to their target audience. With AI, you can provide a **book titling service** that delivers creative, market-tested titles and subtitles based on genre, message, tone, and audience—saving writers hours of frustration and unlocking the clarity they need to launch with confidence.

What You'll Do

You'll use AI to:

- Brainstorm 10–50 potential book titles and subtitles
- Categorize suggestions by tone (serious, playful, motivational, etc.)
- Analyze genre trends to suggest titles that fit the market
- Create unique combinations of keywords, metaphors, and hooks
- Offer subtitle variations based on clarity, SEO, or audience promise

Example prompt:

"Create 25 possible book titles and subtitles for a Christian women's devotional about trusting God during hard times. Include emotional, poetic, and bold options."

"Suggest 20 nonfiction book titles for an entrepreneur teaching how to build passive income online. Include subtitle options with benefits and clarity."

Once generated, you'll polish, curate, and present them in:

- A PDF or Google Doc
- A categorized list (with bonus marketing notes)
- A Canva visual mockup for premium packages

Why It Works

Book titles sell books. Period. And most authors go through endless brainstorming sessions, second-guessing themselves for weeks. You're offering a shortcut to clarity—plus emotional relief—and helping them position their book for success.

This is especially helpful for:

- Self-publishing authors

- Coaches writing lead-generation books
- Faith-based writers seeking deeper meaning in their titles
- Course creators turning content into books

Where to Sell or Promote

- **Fiverr & Upwork**: Create a gig for "Book Title + Subtitle Brainstorming"
- **Author Facebook Groups**: These are goldmines—authors always ask for title help
- **Instagram or TikTok**: Share title makeovers or "Which title would you choose?" polls
- **Your Website**: Add this as a mini-service for self-publishers
- **Email List**: Offer it as a fast-turnaround service for nonfiction authors

What You'll Need

- ChatGPT to generate options
- Grammarly to clean and polish
- Canva or Notion to present visual mockups (optional)
- Optional: Book Bolt or Publisher Rocket for light keyword testing

How Much You Can Charge

- **Basic Title Pack (10–20 ideas)**: $50–$100
- **Expanded Pack (40–60 ideas + mockups)**: $150–$300
- **Custom Messaging & Tagline Bundle**: $400+
- **Template Pack for DIY Authors**: $19–$39

Sell 10 packs/month at $150 = $1,500. Or offer a premium bundle to a coach writing their first book = $400–$500/client.

Tips to Stand Out

- Niche by genre or tone: "Christian Book Titles," "Memoir Titling Pack," "Business Book Headline Studio"
- Add subtitle strategy tips or keyword alignment bonuses
- Offer "Title + Back Cover Copy" as a bundled upsell
- Include an AI-generated blurb preview or mockup to help the author visualize their book

52. Create AI-Written Wedding Vows, Speeches, and Toasts for Couples and Guests

Weddings are emotional, high-stakes events—and many people struggle to find the right words. With AI, you can offer **custom vow-writing and speech-writing services** for brides, grooms, best men, maids of honor, officiants, and parents who want to say something meaningful but don't know where to start.

What You'll Do

You'll use AI to:

- Generate heartfelt, funny, or spiritual wedding vows
- Write full speeches for toasts or receptions
- Create personalized officiant scripts
- Craft father/daughter or mother/son dance intros
- Write short love letters for wedding day gifts

Example prompts:

"Write heartfelt wedding vows for a Christian bride who wants to thank God for her husband and promise to honor their marriage covenant."

"Create a funny but touching best man speech for a groom who's been best friends with the speaker since college. Include 1 personal story and a sincere ending."

Once generated, you'll personalize it further using input from the client and deliver in:

- Google Docs or PDFs
- Printable keepsake formats (via Canva)
- Email-ready text or read-aloud format

Why It Works

People want to say something powerful—but weddings are emotional and writing under pressure is hard. You offer them peace of mind and the perfect words for the biggest moments of their life. This is a **high-trust, high-emotion** service with strong referral potential.

And it's also **evergreen**—wedding season never really ends.

Where to Sell or Promote

- **Fiverr & Upwork**: "Wedding Vow and Speech Writer" gigs are in demand year-round
- **Etsy**: Sell vow or speech templates or printable vow booklets
- **Wedding Facebook Groups**: Brides, grooms, and planners are your clients
- **Instagram Reels & TikTok**: Share snippets of vows or speeches you've written (with permission)
- **Your Website**: Offer this as a personalized service with 24–48 hour turnaround

What You'll Need

- ChatGPT for fast, emotional copy generation
- Canva for printable formats or keepsakes
- Google Forms to collect details from clients
- Optional: Use Loom or VoiceNote to record reading versions

How Much You Can Charge

- **Wedding Vows (1 person)**: $50–$100
- **Custom Speech (2–5 minutes)**: $100–$250
- **Officiant Ceremony Script**: $150–$300
- **Printable Bundle (vows + keepsake design)**: $75–$150
- **Template Pack**: $25–$49

Sell 10 vow bundles/month at $100 = $1,000. Or book 5 full-service clients at $250 = $1,250/month.

Tips to Stand Out

- Niche your tone: "Faith-Based Vows," "Funny Wedding Speeches," "Emotional Maid of Honor Toasts"
- Offer fast-turnaround options for last-minute clients
- Include a personalization checklist to guide people through input
- Bundle with printable vow books or thank-you card templates

53. Sell AI-Generated LinkedIn Carousel Posts for Business Owners and Thought Leaders

Carousel posts are one of the best-performing content types on LinkedIn—but they're time-consuming to plan and write. With AI, you can create **high-value carousel content** that helps business owners grow their influence, showcase expertise, and get more engagement on LinkedIn.

What You'll Do

You'll use AI to:

- Generate 5–10 slide posts on a specific topic (business, leadership, mindset, sales, faith + business, etc.)
- Write attention-grabbing hook slides
- Break down key insights into short, punchy slides
- Include strong CTAs on the final slide
- Add post caption text to accompany each carousel

Example prompts:

"Write a 7-slide LinkedIn carousel for a Christian entrepreneur on the topic 'Why Obedience Leads to Overflow.' Each slide should teach one key idea in under 40 words."

"Create a 10-slide LinkedIn carousel on '5 Ways to Repurpose Your Podcast Content.' Include a hook, 5 strategies, and a call-to-action."

Then, you can format these into:

- Google Docs (text-only version)
- Canva templates (pre-designed and editable)
- PDF ready-to-upload carousels (with client branding if custom)

Why It Works

LinkedIn is exploding with opportunity, and carousels get high reach. But most professionals don't have time or creative energy to write short, visual posts that teach and convert.

You're providing content that positions them as a thought leader—without them having to write it.

Perfect for:

- Coaches and consultants
- Course creators

- Authors and speakers
- Faith-based business leaders
- Small agency owners

Where to Sell or Promote

- **Fiverr & Upwork**: Offer "LinkedIn Carousel Copywriting and Design"
- **Instagram or LinkedIn**: Share carousel examples to attract leads
- **Facebook Groups**: Pitch to thought leaders or business coaches
- **Gumroad or Etsy**: Sell template packs by niche
- **Your Website**: Offer a subscription or bundle of 4–12 carousels/month

What You'll Need

ChatGPT to write the copy

- Canva to design branded carousels
- Google Docs to deliver plain-text scripts
- Optional: ConvertKit or Flodesk if bundling with email content

How Much You Can Charge

- **Text-Only Carousel Copy (per post)**: $30–$60
- **Branded Carousel Design + Copy**: $100–$200/post
- **Monthly Content Pack (4–8 carousels)**: $300–$800
- **Editable Template Pack**: $29–$59 (for DIY users)

Sell 5 carousel packages/month at $150 = $750. Add 100 template downloads at $39 = $3,900 passive.

Tips to Stand Out

- Offer "Niche Packs": "Faith in Business," "Sales Mindset," "Instagram Growth Carousels"
- Include scheduling tips or content repurposing advice
- Add matching captions and hashtags
- Bundle with your **LinkedIn optimization service (#22)** or **newsletter sequences (#35)**

54. Use AI to Create "Done-for-You" Freebie Funnels for Coaches and Digital Sellers

Everyone in the digital space knows they *need* a freebie to grow their list—but few have the time or skill to create a compelling offer, write the copy, and build the funnel. With AI, you can create and sell **ready-to-launch freebie funnels** that include the lead magnet, emails, and landing page copy—all done for them.

What You'll Do

You'll use AI to generate:

- The actual freebie (PDF, checklist, mini guide, etc.)
- Landing page headline, subhead, and opt-in copy
- Thank-you page messaging or upsell suggestion
- 3–5 email follow-up sequence (nurture + pitch)
- Optional: Social captions or promo posts to drive traffic

Example prompts:

"Write a freebie funnel for a Christian life coach helping women overcome fear. Include a 5-step guide as the lead magnet, landing page copy, and 4 follow-up emails."

"Create a lead magnet funnel for a productivity consultant selling a $97 Notion template. Include checklist opt-in, email nurture, and a soft pitch email."

You can package this as:

- A ready-to-use Google Doc bundle
- A Canva-designed funnel with editable copy
- A complete Kajabi or ConvertKit setup (for premium clients)

Why It Works

Freebie funnels are the *engine* of online business growth—but writing them is overwhelming for most solo entrepreneurs. Your service removes the overwhelm and replaces it with clarity, structure, and speed.

This makes you instantly valuable to:

- Coaches
- Course creators
- Etsy or Gumroad sellers

- Faith-based entrepreneurs
- Digital service providers

Where to Sell or Offer It

- **Fiverr & Upwork**: "Done-for-You Freebie Funnel Setup"
- **Facebook Groups**: Pitch to coaches, creators, and digital product sellers
- **Your Website**: Create a portfolio of funnel types and niche examples
- **Email Lists**: Offer pre-built or custom funnel packages
- **Instagram Reels or TikTok**: Show a visual breakdown of what's inside a successful funnel

What You'll Need

- ChatGPT to generate all written content
- Canva to design lead magnets and page visuals
- Google Docs or Notion to deliver bundle files
- Optional: Familiarity with ConvertKit, MailerLite, or Flodesk to help with setup

How Much You Can Charge

- **Freebie + Copy Only**: $100–$200
- **Freebie + Email Sequence + Landing Page Copy**: $300–$500
- **Full Funnel Build (Copy + Design + Setup)**: $700–$1,500
- **Template Pack (DIY funnel kits)**: $39–$89

4 full clients/month at $500 = $2,000. 100 template sales at $49 = $4,900 in passive income.

Tips to Stand Out

- Offer niche-specific funnels: "Faith-Based Freebies for Coaches," "Funnel Kits for Etsy Sellers," "Freebie Funnel for Digital Planners"
- Include bonus launch copy or Canva promo templates
- Provide "Plug-and-Paste" doc format for easy edits
- Bundle with your **email sequences (#43)** or **lead magnet service (#26)**

55. Sell AI-Written Audio Devotionals and Meditations for Faith-Based Creators

Audio devotionals and meditations are exploding in popularity—especially for busy believers who want spiritual encouragement on the go. With AI, you can write **ready-to-record audio devotionals** for Christian influencers, coaches, YouTubers, or ministries who want to launch a podcast, create bonus content, or sell spiritual audio packs.

What You'll Do

You'll use AI to generate:

- Short devotional scripts (2–5 minutes long)
- Guided meditations based on scripture
- Thematic audio series (e.g., peace, healing, purpose)
- Prayer + reflection combinations
- Closing affirmations or journaling prompts

Example prompts:

"Write a 4-minute audio devotional for Christian entrepreneurs about trusting God when business is slow. Include a key scripture, reflection, and prayer."

"Create 7 audio meditations for women healing from heartbreak. Each should include a scripture-based affirmation, a calming message, and a short prayer."

You can sell these as:

- Script-only downloads for creators to record
- Pre-recorded audio files (if you narrate or partner with a voice actor)
- Bundled devotional packs (text + audio)
- Podcast launch kits for faith-based clients

Why It Works

Faith-based creators are looking for new ways to connect with their audience—and audio content builds intimacy. You're giving them the words they need to minister, motivate, or monetize through short-form spiritual content that feels deeply personal.

It's perfect for:

- Podcasters
- Christian coaches and influencers
- YouTube devotionals

- Churches and ministries
- App creators or Christian wellness brands

Where to Sell or Promote

- **Fiverr & Upwork**: "Devotional Script Writing" or "Christian Audio Meditation Writing"
- **Faith-Based Facebook Groups**: Coaches, speakers, and ministers are your audience
- **Etsy or Gumroad**: Sell digital devotional packs or script bundles
- **Your Website**: Offer scriptwriting as a service, or sell pre-written series
- **Instagram or TikTok**: Share audio clips or spoken devotionals for engagement

What You'll Need

- ChatGPT for scriptwriting
- Google Docs or Canva for delivery
- Optional: Voice-over partner or text-to-speech tool for audio
- Optional: Audacity or Descript if editing audio files yourself

How Much You Can Charge

- **Single Devotional Script**: $25–$50
- **7-Day Series (scripts only)**: $100–$250
- **Pre-Recorded Audio Packs**: $150–$400
- **Custom Podcast Devotional Kit**: $500–$1,000+
- **Template/Script Pack for DIY Creators**: $29–$59

Sell 100 packs at $39 = $3,900. Or work with 5 podcasters/month at $250 = $1,250 recurring.

Tips to Stand Out

- Niche your themes: "Faith in Business," "Overcoming Anxiety," "Morning Declarations for Christian Women"
- Bundle with reflection journals or printable affirmation cards
- Offer matching titles and descriptions for podcast uploads
- Create seasonal packs: "Holy Week Devotionals," "21 Days of Focus," "Advent Audio Meditations"

56. Use AI to Write and Sell Classroom Worksheets and Lesson Plans for Teachers

Teachers are constantly searching for engaging, standards-based lesson materials. With AI, you can create and sell **classroom worksheets, lesson plans, and learning activities** tailored to specific subjects, grade levels, and even faith-based curricula. It's a high-demand, low-overhead niche with consistent year-round traffic.

What You'll Do

You'll use AI to generate:

- Reading comprehension worksheets
- Math problem sets with answer keys
- Writing prompts and grammar exercises
- Science, history, or Bible study lessons
- Faith-based curriculum supplements (Christian schools/homeschoolers)

Example prompts:

"Create a 5th grade reading comprehension worksheet based on the parable of the Good Samaritan. Include vocabulary, questions, and a reflection activity."

"Write a science lesson plan for 7th graders about ecosystems. Include objectives, an activity, and quiz questions."

You'll then format the content using:

- Google Docs or Microsoft Word
- Canva (for printable worksheet design)
- PDF exports for selling or sharing

Why It Works

Teachers (especially homeschoolers and faith-based educators) are constantly buying or downloading worksheets to save prep time. You're solving a daily problem with ready-to-use, engaging materials. It's perfect for:

- TeachersPayTeachers (TPT)
- Etsy printable sellers
- Homeschool groups
- Christian schools
- Private tutors

Where to Sell or Promote

- **TeachersPayTeachers (TPT)**: The #1 marketplace for classroom materials
- **Etsy**: Sell bundles for homeschool or Sunday school
- **Gumroad or Payhip**: Create a low-cost storefront for digital downloads
- **Facebook Groups**: Homeschool, Christian education, and teacher groups
- **Your Website**: Offer free downloads to build your list and upsell full packs

What You'll Need

- ChatGPT to create worksheets, quizzes, and lesson content
- Canva or Google Docs to format worksheets and answer keys
- TeachersPayTeachers or Etsy account
- Optional: Trello or Airtable to organize product creation and bundles

How Much You Can Charge

- **Single Worksheet (with answer key)**: $3–$7
- **Lesson Pack (5–10 worksheets)**: $12–$25
- **Monthly Theme Bundles**: $25–$49
- **Yearlong Curriculum (by subject)**: $99–$249

Sell 100 worksheet packs at $19 = $1,900. Add 5 homeschool families on a $29/month subscription = $145/month recurring.

Tips to Stand Out

- Niche your subjects: "Bible-Based Grammar Practice," "Faith-Focused STEM," "Reading Comprehension for Christian Kids"
- Include scripture tie-ins or character-building reflections
- Offer seasonal or holiday-themed packs
- Bundle with activity books, coloring pages, or digital devotionals

57. Offer AI-Generated Client Onboarding Kits for Coaches and Service Providers

A smooth onboarding experience builds trust, reduces confusion, and makes clients feel confident in their investment. With AI, you can create **custom client onboarding kits** for coaches, consultants, and freelancers that include everything from welcome messages to intake forms—all polished and ready to send.

What You'll Do

You'll use AI to generate:

- Personalized welcome letters or emails
- Coaching agreements or client expectations
- Intake forms and pre-session questionnaires
- Onboarding checklists
- Session prep guides or "how to get the most out of this experience" docs

Example prompts:

"Write a client onboarding email for a Christian life coach. Include a welcome message, how to prepare for sessions, and a link to an intake form."

"Create an onboarding kit for a business consultant helping clients scale to 7-figures. Include an expectation agreement, scheduling info, and mindset prep."

Once generated, you can organize it all in:

- Google Docs or PDFs
- Canva-designed client kits
- Trello or Notion templates (for premium digital delivery)

Why It Works

Service providers often wing their onboarding—or forget how critical those first impressions are. Your kit makes them look professional, sets boundaries, and saves time with every new client. Once you've built a few frameworks, it's easy to rinse and repeat.

It's perfect for:

- Life and business coaches
- Virtual assistants and consultants

- Faith-based mentors
- Freelancers in design, marketing, or writing
- Course creators offering 1-on-1 support

Where to Sell or Offer It

- **Fiverr & Upwork**: "Client Onboarding Document Creation" or "Done-for-You Onboarding System"
- **Facebook Groups**: Coaches and VAs are constantly looking for systems like this
- **Instagram or LinkedIn**: Share carousel posts breaking down "what's in your onboarding kit"
- **Gumroad or Etsy**: Sell template bundles by industry or niche
- **Your Website**: Offer as a custom service or plug-and-play download

What You'll Need

- ChatGPT to generate all onboarding content
- Canva or Google Docs to format and brand it
- Optional: Typeform or Google Forms for intake forms
- Trello or Notion if delivering as a digital board or system

How Much You Can Charge

- **Basic Kit (email + form)**: $75–$150
- **Full Kit (5+ pieces + design)**: $250–$500
- **Template Packs (editable)**: $39–$89
- **Custom Trello/Notion Dashboard**: $300–$600+

Sell 5 custom onboarding systems/month at $300 = $1,500. Add 100 template downloads at $49 = $4,900.

Tips to Stand Out

- Niche down: "Onboarding Kits for Christian Coaches," "VAs Serving Agencies," "Onboarding for Spiritual Mentorship Programs"
- Include a bonus "Client Exit Survey" or "Progress Tracker"
- Add client gifting or welcome card templates for a luxury experience
- Bundle with your **Freebie Funnel (#54)** or **Email Welcome Sequences (#43)**

58. Use AI to Write and Sell Product Launch Announcements and Countdown Campaigns

Launching a new product—whether it's a digital download, a course, or a physical item—requires more than just posting "It's live!" With AI, you can create **pre-written launch announcement campaigns** that build hype, create urgency, and guide followers or subscribers toward making a purchase.

What You'll Do

You'll use AI to generate:

- Teaser posts and curiosity-building messages
- Countdown emails (3, 5, or 7-day launch series)
- Launch day email and social captions
- Scarcity/urgency messages ("Last chance," "Cart closes tonight!")
- Post-launch follow-up emails or thank-yous

Example prompts:

"Create a 5-day email countdown sequence for a Christian author launching her new devotional eBook. Include a blend of inspiration and urgency."

"Write a social media launch campaign for a coach releasing a $97 Canva template bundle. Include pre-launch teasers, launch day posts, and urgency messages."

You'll format the content as:

- Google Docs or Notion launch kits
- Canva-designed email swipe files
- Editable social caption bundles
- Email automation plug-and-play templates

Why It Works

Most creators launch too softly. A strategic launch sequence boosts anticipation, builds emotional connection, and drives urgency—which means *more sales*. You're helping clients show up confidently and sell without being pushy.

This is perfect for:

- Etsy or Gumroad sellers

- Coaches launching courses or templates
- Christian authors and speakers
- Digital product creators
- Shopify sellers with seasonal drops

Where to Sell or Offer It

- **Fiverr & Upwork**: "Product Launch Email & Social Campaigns"
- **Facebook Groups**: Coaches, authors, Etsy sellers—goldmine for launch support
- **Your Website**: Create niche launch packs by industry
- **Instagram or TikTok**: Share snippets of your launch copy as samples
- **Email List**: Offer a "Launch Copy Kit" freebie to upsell full service

What You'll Need

- ChatGPT to write high-converting, niche-aligned copy
- Google Docs or Canva to format launch kits
- Optional: Familiarity with ConvertKit, Flodesk, or MailerLite for automation guidance
- Optional: Trello or ClickUp to organize launch timelines

How Much You Can Charge

- **Basic 3-Email Launch Kit**: $100–$200
- **Full 5–7 Email + Social Campaign**: $300–$600
- **Custom Launch Strategy + Copy**: $750–$1,200+
- **Template Pack (for DIY sellers)**: $39–$89

Sell 10 launch kits at $250 = $2,500. Or land 5 high-end clients at $750 = $3,750/month.

Tips to Stand Out

- Niche your kits: "Faith-Based Devotional Launch," "Template Shop Kickoff," "Coaching Program Countdown"
- Offer copy bundles with launch timelines or planning guides
- Include email subject lines, emojis, and CTA tips
- Bundle with your **Freebie Funnel (#54)** or **Email Sequences (#43)** for a full pre-launch setup

59. Sell AI-Generated Brand Story Pages for Websites and Sales Funnels

Every brand needs a compelling origin story—but most business owners struggle to write theirs in a way that's clear, emotional, and persuasive. With AI, you can offer **done-for-you brand story writing services** that help entrepreneurs, coaches, and product creators craft powerful About pages and "Our Story" sections for websites, funnels, and bios.

What You'll Do

You'll use AI to:

- Write personal or brand origin stories
- Structure a clear narrative with emotion, credibility, and a CTA
- Create "About Me" sections for coaches, influencers, and sellers
- Format longer "Our Story" pages for product brands or ministries
- Craft bios for speaking engagements or podcast appearances

Example prompts:

"Write a heartfelt About Me page for a Christian life coach who left her corporate job to follow God's calling and help women find purpose through faith."

"Create a brand story for a skincare brand founded by two sisters who wanted clean, faith-friendly products for sensitive skin. Include origin, mission, and what makes the brand different."

You can package the result as:

- Google Docs for website copy
- Canva-designed one-pagers for media kits
- Funnel-ready bios and story snippets
- Editable templates with multiple formats

Why It Works

Story sells. People buy from brands they connect with—and your service gives them words that inspire trust, spark emotion, and invite action. Great brand stories boost conversion rates, create relatability, and strengthen positioning across all platforms.

Perfect for:

- Coaches and consultants

- Product-based businesses
- Nonprofits and ministries
- Course creators and authors
- Personal brands and influencers

Where to Sell or Offer It

- **Fiverr & Upwork**: "Write Your Brand Story or About Page"
- **Facebook Groups**: Coaches, Etsy sellers, and faith-based entrepreneurs
- **Instagram or LinkedIn**: Share brand storytelling tips and samples
- **Your Website**: Offer as a signature copywriting service
- **Gumroad or Etsy**: Sell plug-and-play brand story templates

What You'll Need

- ChatGPT to generate drafts and structure story arcs
- Google Docs or Canva for formatting and delivery
- Optional: Grammarly for voice consistency and polish
- Optional: Intake form or questionnaire to collect client backstory

How Much You Can Charge

- **Basic About Me Page**: $100–$200
- **Full Brand Story Page**: $250–$500
- **Premium Story + Funnel Copy Package**: $750+
- **DIY Template Pack**: $39–$79

Sell 10 stories at $250 = $2,500. Add 100 template downloads at $49 = $4,900 passive income.

Tips to Stand Out

- Offer "Faith-Based Brand Story Writing" or "Purpose-Driven Brand Bios"
- Include visual formatting or mockups for how it looks on a real site
- Add mission/vision statement creation as a bonus
- Bundle with **Lead Magnet Copy (#26)**, **Welcome Emails (#43)**, or **Sales Page Writing**

60. Use AI to Create and Sell Vision and Mission Statement Templates for Faith-Based Businesses

Many Christian entrepreneurs and ministries have big callings—but struggle to clearly express their **vision** and **mission** in writing. With AI, you can help them define who they are, what they do, and why it matters by offering **done-for-you vision and mission statement services or templates.**

What You'll Do

You'll use AI to generate:

- Powerful mission statements aligned with scripture or purpose
- Clear, compelling vision statements that cast long-term goals
- Core values and brand belief summaries
- Ministry mottos or taglines
- Statement templates for nonprofits, ministries, and Christian brands

Example prompts:

"Write a mission and vision statement for a Christian entrepreneur who helps women build businesses rooted in faith, family, and financial freedom."

"Create a values-based brand belief summary for a nonprofit helping formerly incarcerated men rebuild their lives through the gospel."

You can package these in:

- Google Docs for website or proposal use
- Canva one-pagers for brand decks
- Trello or Notion templates for ongoing brand clarity
- Editable PDF workbooks for teams and ministries

Why It Works

A mission and vision statement isn't just a formality—it's fuel. It guides decisions, unites teams, and sets the tone for marketing and ministry. But most people either overcomplicate it or copy from someone else. Your AI-powered service offers fast clarity, spiritual alignment, and professionalism.

Perfect for:

- Christian entrepreneurs and coaches

- Faith-based nonprofits and ministries
- Course creators and personal brands
- Small business owners building value-led companies

Where to Sell or Offer It

- **Fiverr & Upwork**: "Mission & Vision Statement Copy for Christian Brands"
- **Facebook Groups**: Christian entrepreneurship, ministry, and coaching circles
- **Instagram or TikTok**: Share breakdowns of powerful faith-filled mission statements
- **Your Website**: Add to your brand development or messaging services
- **Etsy or Gumroad**: Sell a vision/mission workbook or template pack

What You'll Need

- ChatGPT to generate compelling, personalized statements
- Google Docs, Notion, or Canva for delivery
- Optional: Intake form to gather brand beliefs, calling, and audience

How Much You Can Charge

- **Mission & Vision Statement (Custom)**: $75–$150
- **Full Brand Identity Pack (Vision + Mission + Values)**: $200–$400
- **Workbooks & Template Packs**: $25–$49
- **Faith-Based Business Starter Kit**: $99–$149

Sell 5 brand identity packs at $300 = $1,500/month. Or 100 workbook downloads at $39 = $3,900 in passive income.

Tips to Stand Out

- Niche down: "For Christian Coaches," "For Nonprofits," "For Faith-Based Startups"
- Offer a free mission statement template as a lead magnet
- Bundle with **Brand Story Copy (#59)**, **Tagline Writing**, or **Website About Page Services**
- Include optional scripture alignment or verse inspiration for each statement

61. Offer AI-Generated Speaker Bios and Event Intros for Public Figures and Thought Leaders

Whether someone is speaking at a church, conference, workshop, or podcast, they need a strong, concise **speaker bio** and **event introduction**. With AI, you can write professional, inspiring, and audience-specific bios that help speakers communicate their credibility and connect with listeners immediately.

What You'll Do

You'll use AI to generate:

- 100–200 word professional bios for websites, speaking packets, or press kits
- Short 1-paragraph intros for hosts to read aloud before the speaker takes the stage
- 3rd-person and 1st-person versions for versatility
- Optional tagline or "signature message" statements
- Bio bundles for podcast guests, conferences, or summits

Example prompts:

"Write a speaker bio for a Christian author who teaches women how to grow in faith and launch purpose-driven businesses. Keep it professional, warm, and under 150 words."

"Create a conference host intro for a keynote speaker discussing spiritual healing and identity. Include one personal fact, their ministry role, and a compelling final line to welcome them."

You'll deliver in:

- Google Docs or Canva-designed bios
- PDF media kit pages
- Editable text files for easy updates

Why It Works

Many amazing speakers freeze when it's time to talk about themselves. Your service gives them clarity, confidence, and consistency across their platforms—plus a professional edge when applying for events or interviews.

This is perfect for:

- Christian speakers and ministers

- Authors and podcast hosts
- Coaches and consultants
- Workshop and webinar hosts
- Panelists and summit guests

Where to Sell or Offer It

- **Fiverr & Upwork**: "Speaker Bio & Event Introduction Writing"
- **Facebook Groups**: Christian women in leadership, speaker networks, author groups
- **Instagram or LinkedIn**: Share bio makeovers and before/after examples
- **Your Website**: Offer this as a standalone or bundled service
- **Email List**: Offer free tips + upsell a full service

What You'll Need

- ChatGPT to generate bios and intros
- Google Docs or Canva for formatting
- Optional: Client intake form with audience, tone, and personal highlights
- Grammarly or Hemingway to polish delivery

How Much You Can Charge

- **Single Speaker Bio**: $75–$150
- **Speaker Bio + Host Intro**: $150–$300
- **Full Media Kit Bundle**: $350–$600+
- **Bio Template Pack**: $25–$49 for DIY creators

Just 6 clients/month at $150 = $900. Add 100 bio template packs at $39 = $3,900 passive.

Tips to Stand Out

- Niche your offer: "Speaker Bios for Christian Women," "Podcast Guest Bios," "Summit Speaker Packs"
- Include 3 tone options: formal, warm, bold
- Bundle with **LinkedIn Bio (#22)**, **Brand Story (#59)**, or **Mission Statements (#60)**
- Offer a "Done in 48 Hours" fast delivery tier for extra income

62. Use AI to Write High-Converting Testimonials and Case Studies for Clients

Social proof sells—but many clients struggle to **gather or write compelling testimonials** that actually move people to buy. With AI, you can offer a service that turns basic feedback into **powerful testimonials** or full **client success stories**, written in a structured, persuasive format that builds trust and boosts conversions.

What You'll Do

You'll use AI to:

- Reword bland testimonials into engaging social proof
- Turn a short email or review into a polished paragraph
- Create structured case studies (problem → process → result)
- Write video testimonial scripts or prompts for clients to send to their customers
- Format testimonials for websites, sales pages, or product launches

Example prompts:

"Turn this sentence into a compelling testimonial for a Christian mindset coach: 'She really helped me stop doubting myself and hear God's voice again.'"

"Create a case study for a business consultant who helped a client double their revenue in 90 days. Include the challenge, action steps, and outcome with quotes."

Deliver the final product in:

- Google Docs or Canva one-pagers
- Website-ready snippets with HTML formatting
- Slide decks for presentations or pitches
- PDF case study packs with visuals and quotes

Why It Works

Potential customers want *proof.* A great testimonial can do more than a thousand ads—but most businesses don't use them right. You help transform casual feedback into trust-building assets that boost credibility and conversion across websites, emails, and social media.

Ideal for:

- Coaches and consultants
- Digital product sellers

- Agencies, freelancers, or VAs
- Course creators and ministries

Where to Sell or Offer It

- **Fiverr & Upwork**: "Testimonial Writing" or "Client Case Study Copywriting"
- **Facebook Groups**: Coaches, freelancers, or digital product sellers
- **Your Website**: Offer as a conversion copy service
- **Instagram/TikTok**: Share before/after examples of upgraded testimonials
- **Email Lists**: Offer a free template in exchange for list growth and upsell later

What You'll Need

- ChatGPT to reword and polish testimonials
- Google Forms to collect raw client feedback
- Google Docs or Canva to deliver final versions
- Optional: Loom to explain how to use them for video or website placement

How Much You Can Charge

- **Basic Testimonial Upgrade (5–10 lines)**: $50–$100
- **Full Case Study Write-Up**: $200–$500
- **Video Script/Testimonial Prompts**: $75–$150
- **Template Pack for Businesses**: $29–$59

Sell 5 case studies/month at $300 = $1,500. Add 100 template downloads at $39 = $3,900/month passive.

Tips to Stand Out

- Niche your offer: "Faith-Based Coach Testimonial Writing," "Case Studies for Freelancers," "Social Proof Kits for Etsy Sellers"
- Include visual formatting options or Canva templates
- Offer bundles with **Launch Copy (#58)**, **Brand Story (#59)**, or **Funnel Kits (#54)**
- Add "how to collect better testimonials" tip sheets for your clients

63. Use AI to Create Interactive Quiz Funnels for Lead Generation or Digital Product Sales

Quizzes are one of the most effective ways to capture leads and drive sales—but most creators don't know how to write one that converts. With AI, you can build **interactive quiz funnels** that segment users, deliver personalized results, and lead into email lists, product recommendations, or coaching offers.

What You'll Do

You'll use AI to generate:

- Quiz titles and hook questions (e.g. "What's Your Faith-Fueled Business Style?")
- Multiple-choice or personality-based questions
- Branching logic outcomes (e.g., 3–5 result types)
- Personalized result descriptions
- Email opt-in copy + CTA for each result
- Optional: Upsell or product recommendation at the end

Example prompts:

"Create a 7-question quiz for Christian entrepreneurs titled 'What's Your Kingdom Business Identity?' Include results for Visionary, Builder, Teacher, and Shepherd with tailored encouragement and tips."

"Write a quiz funnel for a productivity coach helping moms. Include fun language, nurturing tone, and lead to a free download or $17 product."

You can deliver the quizzes in:

- Google Docs (for copy)
- Set up on platforms like **Interact**, **TryInteract**, **Typeform**, or **Thrive Quiz Builder**
- Canva-designed quiz result pages
- Optional PDF quiz result summaries

Why It Works

Quizzes are interactive, personal, and fun—plus they gather emails like crazy. People LOVE learning about themselves, and these tools help creators **segment their audience**, recommend the right offers, and increase conversions.

Great for:

- Coaches and course creators
- Christian mentors or ministry programs
- Digital product sellers
- Agencies helping clients build lists

Where to Sell or Offer It

- **Fiverr & Upwork**: "Quiz Funnel Writing and Setup"
- **Facebook Groups**: Coaches, consultants, and creators
- **Instagram or TikTok**: Share quiz ideas or results to drive curiosity
- **Your Website**: Offer quiz-building services or templates
- **Email Lists**: Use a free quiz template or quiz swipe file as a lead magnet

What You'll Need

- ChatGPT to write all quiz content and results
- Google Docs or Canva to organize
- Typeform, Interact, or Thrive to build the actual quiz (optional but powerful)
- Optional: ConvertKit or MailerLite to trigger email sequences

How Much You Can Charge

- **Quiz Copy Only**: $150–$300
- **Full Quiz Funnel (Copy + Setup)**: $400–$1,000+
- **Quiz Templates (Editable)**: $29–$59
- **Subscription Model**: $49/month for new quiz templates in different niches

Just 3 full-service quiz clients/month at $500 = $1,500. Sell 100 template kits at $39 = $3,900/month passive.

Tips to Stand Out

- Niche quiz funnels: "Faith-Based Business Personality," "What Type of Coach Are You?", "Which Digital Product Should You Sell?"
- Bundle with **Email Sequences (#43)** or **Freebie Funnel (#54)**
- Include result-based product recommendations or CTA to book a call
- Add a lead magnet version (PDF of results + bonus resource)

64. Sell AI-Written Course Module Descriptions and Curriculum Outlines

Online course creators often get stuck when it's time to describe their content. With AI, you can offer **professional, engaging course descriptions and module outlines** that help educators clearly communicate their value, organize their material, and increase conversions.

What You'll Do

You'll use AI to write:

- Complete course descriptions (for websites, landing pages, or platforms like Teachable or Kajabi)
- Module-by-module outlines with lesson titles and objectives
- Lesson summaries and optional bullet points for learning outcomes
- Short blurbs for use on checkout pages or ads
- Bonus: Certification or transformation statements ("By the end of this course, you will...")

Example prompts:

"Write a course description for a 6-week program helping Christian entrepreneurs overcome fear and step into purpose. Include module titles and a promise of transformation."

"Create an outline for an online course teaching beginners how to build a digital product business. Include 6 modules with 3 lessons each and outcome-based language."

You can format and deliver as:

- Google Docs for editing
- Website-ready copy
- Slide decks for course previews or webinars
- Canva-designed curriculum maps

Why It Works

A clear course outline and powerful description help creators sell more and teach better. You're helping them clarify their offer, reduce refund rates, and boost professionalism—without them spending hours writing it themselves.

Perfect for:

- Coaches launching signature programs

- Faith-based educators or ministries
- Course creators using Teachable, Kajabi, or Podia
- Digital product instructors and consultants

Where to Sell or Offer It

- **Fiverr & Upwork**: "Course Description and Curriculum Writer"
- **Facebook Groups**: Coaches and course creators
- **Instagram or LinkedIn**: Share tips for structuring winning online courses
- **Your Website**: Offer as a conversion copywriting service
- **Gumroad or Etsy**: Sell course outline templates by niche

What You'll Need

- ChatGPT to generate course descriptions and lesson outlines
- Google Docs or Canva for formatting
- Optional: Course hosting knowledge (Kajabi, Thinkific, etc.)
- Grammarly or Hemingway to polish the tone

How Much You Can Charge

- **Course Description Only**: $100–$200
- **Full Module Outline + Description**: $300–$600
- **Premium Copy Package (with bonuses + landing page copy)**: $750–$1,200
- **Template Pack (Editable DIY Course Outlines)**: $29–$79

4 premium clients/month at $500 = $2,000. Sell 100 template kits at $39 = $3,900/month passive.

Tips to Stand Out

- Niche your offer: "Faith-Based Course Outline Services," "Wellness Coaches," "Product Launch Educators"
- Offer bonuses: email announcement copy, lesson slide titles, CTA blurbs
- Include a "Course Mapping Worksheet" for DIY creators
- Bundle with **Email Sequences (#43)**, **Launch Copy (#58)**, or **Quiz Funnels (#63)**

65. Use AI to Write and Sell Canva Bio Link Page Copy for Instagram and TikTok Creators

Most creators and entrepreneurs use services like **Linktree** or **Canva bio link pages** to list their top resources, lead magnets, and products. But they often struggle to write clear, persuasive micro-copy for those buttons, headlines, and blurbs. With AI, you can offer **bio link copywriting and page setup services** that increase conversions and brand clarity in just one link.

What You'll Do

You'll use AI to:

- Write the short bio headline ("Helping Christian moms build businesses from faith, not fear")
- Craft button text (not just "Freebie" but "Grab My 7-Day Faith Planner")
- Write 1-line product or service descriptions
- Create CTA blurbs ("Start your purpose journey here!")
- Organize the layout for easy navigation

Example prompts:

"Write a Link in Bio headline and 5-button descriptions for a Christian author promoting her latest book, free devotional, podcast, and speaking inquiries."

"Create compelling micro-copy for a Canva link-in-bio page for a course creator with a freebie funnel, coaching program, and blog."

You'll deliver the content:

- In Google Docs (for DIY setup)
- As a pre-designed Canva Link in Bio template (editable)
- Or set up the whole thing directly for the client (if you offer Canva Pro services)

Why It Works

First impressions matter. This is the **digital business card** of today—and most people's bio links are messy, confusing, or under-optimized. With your service, they'll get a page that flows, makes sense, and actually *gets clicks*.

Perfect for:

- Christian creators and authors
- Etsy or Gumroad sellers
- Coaches, speakers, and online course creators
- Affiliate marketers and digital product sellers

Where to Sell or Offer It

- **Fiverr & Upwork**: "Link in Bio Copy + Setup"
- **Facebook Groups**: Entrepreneurs, authors, and influencers always ask for this
- **Instagram or TikTok**: Show before/after bio link upgrades in reels
- **Your Website**: Offer as a mini service or bundle
- **Email Lists**: Give away a free bio headline formula to upsell full setup

What You'll Need

- ChatGPT for generating creative button text and blurbs
- Canva to build and brand the actual bio page
- Google Docs for easy delivery
- Optional: Brand guidelines or product links from the client

How Much You Can Charge

- **Copywriting Only**: $75–$150
- **Copy + Canva Bio Page Setup**: $200–$350
- **Full Brand Bio Bundle (Page + IG Bio + CTA Templates)**: $400–$750
- **Bio Page Template Pack**: $29–$59 (passive)

Sell 5 setups/month at $250 = $1,250. Add 100 template sales at $39 = $3,900/month in passive income.

Tips to Stand Out

- Include bonus icons, headshots, or branded button styles in Canva
- Niche down: "Link in Bio Setup for Christian Creators," "Coaches," or "Authors"
- Bundle with **Email Funnel Setup (#54)** or **Lead Magnet Copy (#26)**
- Offer a monthly refresh or holiday promo update as an upsell

66. Offer AI-Written Weekly Social Media Devotionals for Ministries and Christian Brands

Churches, Christian influencers, and faith-based businesses often struggle to post consistently. With AI, you can create **weekly devotional content** formatted for Instagram, Facebook, email, or blogs—offering it as a subscription or digital product that provides consistency, spiritual encouragement, and sharable inspiration.

What You'll Do

You'll use AI to write:

- 52 weekly devotionals (or monthly sets)
- Each post with a scripture, short teaching, and prayer or reflection
- Caption text for social sharing (Instagram, Facebook, etc.)
- Optional: Email version with a subject line and intro
- Optional: Canva graphics with scripture or quotes

Example prompts:

"Write a weekly devotional post for Christian entrepreneurs about staying faithful in dry seasons. Include scripture, a 150-word reflection, and a call to trust God."

"Create 4 devotionals for women struggling with identity. Each should include a Bible verse, encouragement, and prayer."

You'll deliver the content:

- In Google Docs or Notion (organized by week/month)
- As Canva templates or PDF printables
- Via email subscription or membership model

Why It Works

Faith-based brands want to post more—but don't always have the time or words. Your devotional content fills that gap with spiritually rich, ready-to-post encouragement that aligns with their mission.

It also works beautifully as:

- A digital product
- A content club or subscription
- Bonus content for ministry groups or coaching programs

Where to Sell or Promote It

- **Etsy or Gumroad**: Sell monthly or annual devotional packs
- **Fiverr & Upwork**: Offer as "Devotional Content Writing" or "Christian Social Media Posts"
- **Instagram & Facebook**: Show samples or testimonials from ministries using your posts
- **Your Website**: Launch a devotional membership or digital store
- **Email List**: Offer a free 7-day devotional to upsell the full series

What You'll Need

- ChatGPT to write devotionals, reflections, and captions
- Canva to create matching graphics or printable versions
- Google Docs or Notion to organize the series
- Email service if offering as a drip-content subscription

How Much You Can Charge

- **Weekly Devotional Packs (PDF or Google Doc)**: $19–$49/month
- **Full Year Pack (52 Weeks)**: $149–$249
- **Custom Branded Devotionals for Ministries**: $500–$1,000
- **Subscription Model**: $15–$39/month recurring

Sell 100 year-long devotional packs at $149 = $14,900. Or build 50 subscribers at $29/month = $1,450/month recurring.

Tips to Stand Out

- Niche your content: "For Christian Women," "For Entrepreneurs," "For Youth Ministries," "For Couples"
- Offer scripture-based affirmation versions or journaling prompts
- Bundle with **Canva Templates, Email Sequences (#43)**, or **Planner Inserts**
- Include seasonal packs: "Advent Devotionals," "Faith & Focus for the New Year," etc.

67. Sell AI-Written Google Business Profile Content and Reviews Strategy Kits

Local businesses often neglect their **Google Business Profile**—and yet, it's one of the most powerful tools for attracting customers. With AI, you can write **optimized business descriptions, service blurbs, review responses, and posting strategies** that help small business owners look professional, rank higher, and win trust online.

What You'll Do

You'll use AI to:

- Write keyword-rich business descriptions (up to 750 characters)
- Create service descriptions for each offering
- Generate 10–20 Google Business "Posts" (offers, updates, events)
- Write thank-you and response templates for customer reviews
- Build FAQs with answers based on common search terms

Example prompts:

"Write a 750-character Google Business Profile description for a Christian barbershop that highlights community, professionalism, and faith-based values."

"Create 10 Google Posts for a small bakery, including seasonal offers, behind-the-scenes updates, and weekend promotions."

Deliverables can include:

- Google Docs with editable text
- Canva graphics for Google Posts
- Copy-and-paste review responses
- Setup instructions or checklists for business owners

Why It Works

Google Business listings are *often the first thing* someone sees when they search for a business—but most small business owners don't know how to optimize them. You're offering a way to stand out, attract more reviews, and boost local visibility—with minimal effort on their part.

This is ideal for:

- Barbershops, salons, churches, and realtors
- Local restaurants, coffee shops, tutors, and tradespeople

- Freelancers or digital agencies offering local services
- Faith-based businesses wanting to share their message professionally

Where to Sell or Offer It

- **Fiverr & Upwork**: "Google My Business Content Creation"
- **Facebook Groups**: Small business, Christian entrepreneur, or local chamber communities
- **Local Networking Events**: Offer it as part of your digital marketing help
- **Your Website**: Sell the kits or offer setup services
- **Email Lists**: Promote with a free Google Business Checklist to upsell your kit

What You'll Need

- ChatGPT for writing descriptions, posts, and review responses
- Google Docs or Notion for deliverables
- Canva for simple post graphics (optional)
- Optional: Google Business experience (but not required for copy-only service)

How Much You Can Charge

- **Basic Optimization Pack (description + services)**: $100–$200
- **Content Pack (10–20 posts + reviews + responses)**: $250–$500
- **Full Setup + Strategy Kit**: $600–$1,000+
- **Template Bundle**: $39–$79 (DIY small biz owners)

Just 5 local clients at $400/month = $2,000. Or 100 template sales at $49 = $4,900 in passive revenue.

Tips to Stand Out

- Offer bundles: "Local Business Visibility Kit," "Faith-Based Google Optimization Kit"
- Provide a bonus "How to Get More Reviews" email/script
- Include Canva post templates with pre-written captions
- Pair this with **Brand Bio Writing (#59)** or **Testimonial Strategy (#62)**

68. Offer AI-Written Refund Policies, Terms, and FAQs for Digital Product Creators

Most digital product sellers skip writing proper **refund policies**, **terms of use**, and **FAQs**—or worse, they copy someone else's. With AI, you can offer clear, brand-aligned, and legally aware (but not legal advice) copy that protects their business, sets expectations, and boosts buyer confidence.

What You'll Do

You'll use AI to:

- Write refund and return policies (for digital vs. physical products)
- Draft simple terms and conditions that explain usage rights
- Create clear FAQ sections for product pages or sales funnels
- Add disclaimers (e.g., "not a substitute for professional advice")
- Customize based on industry, tone, and audience

Example prompts:

"Write a friendly refund policy for a Christian course creator selling digital devotionals. Emphasize no refunds on downloads, but offer customer support if there's an issue."

"Create FAQs for a digital planner shop, including questions about editing, device compatibility, and instant downloads."

You'll deliver the content as:

- Google Docs or Word documents
- Website-ready text for product listings
- Canva-designed FAQ cards for social use
- Optional: Upload-ready policy pages (if offering site help)

Why It Works

Setting boundaries builds trust. Clear policies protect creators from confusion, reduce refund requests, and help customers feel confident. You're saving clients *time, headaches, and money* by giving them professional, conversion-boosting language.

Ideal for:

- Etsy and Gumroad sellers

- Course creators and coaches
- Christian content creators
- Shopify sellers or Notion template shops

Where to Sell or Offer It

- **Fiverr & Upwork**: "Refund Policy, Terms, and FAQ Writing"
- **Facebook Groups**: Digital product sellers and course creators
- **Instagram/TikTok**: Share FAQ examples or refund policy tips
- **Your Website**: Bundle as part of a "Shop Copywriting" package
- **Etsy or Gumroad**: Sell plug-and-play templates or policy kits

What You'll Need

- ChatGPT to generate policies, terms, and FAQs
- Google Docs for easy delivery
- Optional: Canva or PDF formatting for template sales
- Optional: Website builder access for setup support

How Much You Can Charge

- **Single Policy (Refund or Terms)**: $75–$125
- **Full Shop Policy & FAQ Pack**: $200–$400
- **Site/Store Setup + Policy Bundle**: $500–$800+
- **Template Pack (DIY)**: $25–$49

Sell 100 template packs at $39 = $3,900. Land 4 full-service clients/month at $350 = $1,400.

Tips to Stand Out

- Focus on digital sellers: "Policies for Printable Shops," "Course Creator Compliance Kit"
- Offer friendly, faith-aligned tone options (firm but gracious)
- Include bonus "How to Handle Difficult Customers" email responses
- Bundle with **Product Description Copy (#36)** or **Email Response Templates (#43)**

69. Sell AI-Written Inspirational Quote Packs for Content Creators and Faith-Based Brands

Everyone loves a good quote—but finding the right one for your audience, writing it from scratch, or pairing it with scripture takes time. With AI, you can create and sell **quote packs** that are motivational, faith-centered, niche-specific, and perfect for daily posting, printing, or pairing with digital products.

What You'll Do

You'll use AI to generate:

- Original motivational or faith-based quotes
- Scripture-inspired affirmations
- Quote series by topic (e.g. healing, purpose, patience, love, courage)
- Caption-ready blurbs to go with each quote
- Optional: Matching Canva graphics or printable quote cards

Example prompts:

"Write 30 original inspirational quotes for Christian entrepreneurs building their business by faith, not fear."

"Create 50 quotes themed around healing and restoration, written in an uplifting, devotional tone. Include a short reflection for each."

You'll deliver your packs as:

- Google Docs or editable PDFs
- Canva templates (square graphics, stories, pins)
- Printable cards, planner inserts, or journaling prompts

Why It Works

Quotes are *shareable, snackable, and powerful*. Content creators, coaches, and brands need constant inspiration to fill their feeds. You provide high-value, consistent content they can post or use—without having to write a thing.

Perfect for:

- Christian influencers and social media managers
- Etsy printable shop owners
- Coaches, speakers, and authors
- Faith-based blogs or newsletters

Where to Sell or Promote It

- **Etsy & Gumroad**: Perfect for digital downloads and printable packs
- **Fiverr**: Offer quote writing, bundles, or branded sets
- **Facebook Groups**: Christian creators, IG content groups, and coaches
- **Instagram Reels or Pinterest**: Post snippets and link to shop
- **Your Website**: Launch a "Content Vault" with ongoing quote drops

What You'll Need

- ChatGPT for generating quotes, captions, or scripture pairings
- Canva for graphics or card designs
- Google Docs or PDFs for organizing the pack
- Optional: Use categories or color-coding for printable bundles

How Much You Can Charge

- **30-Quote Text Pack**: $9–$19
- **50-Quote Canva + Text Pack**: $29–$49
- **100-Quote Printable Pack**: $59–$99
- **Monthly Quote Club Subscription**: $15–$29/month

Sell 100 packs at $29 = $2,900/month. 50 subscribers at $25/month = $1,250 in recurring income.

Tips to Stand Out

- Niche deep: "Quotes for Christian Moms," "Bold Quotes for Kingdom CEOs," "Scripture-Rooted Affirmations for Anxiety"
- Bundle with **Social Captions (#45)**, **Devotionals (#66)**, or **Planners (#40)**
- Offer both editable and graphic versions
- Add "Done-for-You Reels Templates" using the quotes for an upsell

70. Sell AI-Written Blog Post Templates and SEO-Ready Article Starters

Many online business owners know they *should* be blogging to grow traffic and trust—but they don't know where to start. With AI, you can offer **blog post templates** and **starter packs** that help creators, coaches, and Christian entrepreneurs write faster, rank higher, and publish consistently without overwhelm.

What You'll Do

You'll use AI to generate:

- SEO-optimized blog post outlines (titles, headers, and intros)
- 500–800 word starter posts with space for customization
- Call-to-action suggestions for the end of each post
- Suggested keywords and tags
- Optional: Title variations, meta descriptions, and Pinterest pin captions

Example prompts:

"Write an SEO-optimized blog post outline for a Christian money coach on 'How to Budget with Biblical Wisdom.' Include a hook, 5 subheadings, and a CTA."

"Create a 750-word blog post draft for a productivity coach titled 'Why You're Not Lazy—You're Just Misaligned.' Include space for personal story and product plug."

You can package your blog templates as:

- Google Docs with customizable content
- Canva PDFs for planners or printable formats
- Editable Notion templates with formatting tips
- Niche-specific bundles or subscription libraries

Why It Works

Blog content builds trust, boosts SEO, and keeps traffic flowing to websites and shops—but writing is time-consuming. Your AI-written blog kits give creators a shortcut to consistent visibility and long-term traffic.

Ideal for:

- Coaches and consultants
- Christian authors and speakers
- Course creators and Etsy shop owners

- Affiliate marketers and digital product sellers

Where to Sell or Promote It

- **Fiverr & Upwork**: "Blog Post Template Creation" or "AI-Optimized Blog Drafts"
- **Etsy & Gumroad**: Sell niche packs or planners
- **Facebook Groups**: Bloggers, Christian business owners, digital creators
- **Instagram or LinkedIn**: Share "blog starter" swipe files or tips
- **Your Website**: Offer a content starter library or SEO blog kit

What You'll Need

- ChatGPT for generating drafts, outlines, and CTA ideas
- Google Docs or Notion for organizing
- Canva if offering printable or planner-style formats
- Optional: Ubersuggest or Keywords Everywhere for SEO ideas

How Much You Can Charge

- **Single Blog Starter + SEO Outline**: $50–$100
- **Blog Content Pack (4–5 posts)**: $200–$400
- **Monthly Blog Subscription**: $49–$99/month
- **DIY Template Pack (Editable)**: $25–$59

Sell 100 template kits at $39 = $3,900. 10 monthly subscribers at $79 = $790/month in recurring income.

Tips to Stand Out

- Niche the bundles: "Blog Starters for Faith-Based Coaches," "SEO for Etsy Sellers," "Christian Lifestyle Content Kit"
- Include plug-and-play affiliate link CTA options
- Offer a free starter post as a lead magnet
- Bundle with **Email Copy (#43)**, **Launch Copy (#58)**, or **Product Descriptions (#36)**

71. Offer AI-Powered Content Repurposing Services (Turn One Idea into 10 Pieces)

Most creators struggle with *consistency*—not because they lack ideas, but because they don't know how to stretch one idea across multiple platforms. With AI, you can offer **content repurposing services** that turn 1 video, blog post, podcast episode, or live stream into 5–10 polished pieces of content for social, email, and web.

What You'll Do

You'll use AI to:

- Summarize videos, blogs, or talks into core points
- Create Instagram captions, Reels scripts, and carousels
- Write tweet threads or LinkedIn posts
- Extract quotes for graphics or Pinterest pins
- Turn one blog post into an email or short devotional

Example prompts:

"Turn this 7-minute YouTube video on spiritual entrepreneurship into 1 Instagram caption, 1 email, 1 LinkedIn post, and 3 short-form video scripts."

"Repurpose this blog post about faith-based leadership into a carousel outline, a tweet thread, and a 5-bullet devotional email."

You'll package and deliver:

- Google Docs with labeled content by platform
- Canva graphics or templates (optional)
- Notion or Trello boards for content calendars
- Zip folders with all repurposed copy + visuals

Why It Works

Your clients already have content—they just don't know how to multiply its reach. You're turning their *one-time effort* into evergreen marketing that works across platforms, helping them grow with less burnout.

Perfect for:

- Coaches and Christian creators
- YouTubers and podcasters
- Etsy sellers and course creators

- Pastors, speakers, and authors

Where to Sell or Promote It

- **Fiverr & Upwork**: "Content Repurposing for Creators and Coaches"
- **Facebook Groups**: Especially for content creators, coaches, and course builders
- **Instagram or LinkedIn**: Show "1 idea → 10 content pieces" breakdowns
- **Your Website**: Offer a repurposing package or monthly plan
- **Email List**: Promote as "Done-for-You Consistent Content" help

What You'll Need

- ChatGPT to summarize and repurpose content
- Google Docs or Notion for organizing delivery
- Canva for quote graphics or branded visuals
- Optional: Loom to walk clients through the deliverables

How Much You Can Charge

- **Basic Repurpose Pack (1 video/post)**: $100–$200
- **Expanded Pack (3–5 content pieces)**: $300–$500
- **Monthly Repurposing Plan (4–8 sessions/month)**: $750–$1,200+
- **Template Kit (DIY Repurposing Prompts)**: $39–$59

Sell 4 monthly clients at $500 = $2,000/month. Or sell 100 kits at $39 = $3,900 in passive income.

Tips to Stand Out

- Offer niche packages: "Faith-Based Repurposing," "Coaches with Courses," "Podcaster Content Splintering"
- Include a content calendar or posting checklist
- Bundle with **Quote Packs (#69)**, **Blog Starters (#70)**, or **Email Sequences (#43)**
- Upsell video transcription and AI-enhanced summaries

72. Sell AI-Generated Coaching Session Recap Templates and Progress Trackers

Many coaches and consultants struggle with session follow-ups. They either forget to send them, don't know what to say, or spend too much time writing recaps. With AI, you can offer **session recap templates** and **progress tracking tools** that allow coaches to follow up like pros—saving time and increasing client satisfaction.

What You'll Do

You'll use AI to:

- Create plug-and-play coaching recap templates
- Write example summaries, next steps, and encouragement notes
- Generate accountability check-ins and goal trackers
- Add space for scripture, affirmations, or journaling (for faith-based coaches)
- Build templates for 1-on-1 coaching, group programs, or masterminds

Example prompts:

"Write a session recap template for a Christian mindset coach. Include sections for wins, challenges, scripture encouragement, action steps, and prayer points."

"Create a 4-week client progress tracker for a productivity coach. Include goals, tasks completed, and motivation check-ins."

Deliverables can include:

- Google Docs or fillable PDFs
- Canva-designed coaching kits
- Notion templates or Trello boards
- Editable email templates for post-session delivery

Why It Works

Clients LOVE feeling seen and supported between sessions. Coaches LOVE saving time. These templates help coaches stay organized, look professional, and deepen their client relationships without starting from scratch every week.

Perfect for:

- Life and business coaches
- Faith-based mentors

- Group coaching leaders and masterminds
- Wellness, mindset, or financial coaches

Where to Sell or Offer It

- **Fiverr & Upwork**: "Coaching Session Recap Template Design"
- **Etsy & Gumroad**: Sell as a printable or digital coaching pack
- **Facebook Groups**: Coaches and consultants in need of systems
- **Instagram or TikTok**: Show off the recap workflow in Reels or carousel posts
- **Your Website**: Offer it as a "Client Experience Toolkit" for coaches

What You'll Need

- ChatGPT to generate content templates and recap samples
- Canva, Google Docs, or Notion for formatting and delivery
- Optional: Email service to deliver recap reminders or automations
- Optional: Coaching intake form templates to bundle

How Much You Can Charge

- **Single Recap Template (Editable)**: $25–$49
- **Full Recap + Tracker Kit**: $79–$149
- **Custom Branded Coaching Pack**: $200–$500
- **Subscription or Membership (Monthly Templates)**: $19–$39/month

Sell 100 kits at $49 = $4,900. Add 30 monthly subscribers at $29 = $870/month recurring.

Tips to Stand Out

- Offer niche-specific options: "Christian Life Coach Templates," "Mindset & Business Coach Kits," "High-Ticket Client Tracker Templates"
- Include customizable affirmation banks, scriptures, or reflection prompts
- Bundle with **Onboarding Kits (#57)**, **Email Follow-Ups (#43)**, or **Goal Planners (#40)**
- Provide a video walkthrough or onboarding guide

73. Sell AI-Generated Webinar Scripts and Slide Content for Coaches and Digital Sellers

Webinars are powerful sales tools—but creating the **script**, **slide content**, and **CTA structure** is overwhelming for most people. With AI, you can deliver ready-to-use webinar frameworks that make it easy for creators to educate, inspire, and sell without struggling to organize their thoughts.

What You'll Do

You'll use AI to generate:

- Complete webinar outlines with intro, teaching, and offer sections
- Word-for-word presenter scripts (or bullet-style if preferred)
- Slide content (titles, bullet points, stories, CTA prompts)
- Story prompts, teaching frameworks, and objection-handling lines
- Optional: Email reminders or follow-ups tied to the webinar funnel

Example prompts:

"Write a 45-minute webinar script for a Christian business coach teaching 'How to Start a Kingdom-Based Business.' Include a 3-part teaching, scripture references, and a soft pitch at the end."

"Create slide content for a productivity expert hosting a free masterclass on time-blocking. Include teaching points, stats, and a 3-slide offer section."

You'll deliver the content in:

- Google Docs (script)
- Canva or PowerPoint slide templates
- Editable Notion outline (for DIY course creators)
- Full webinar funnel kit (if bundled)

Why It Works

Webinars are one of the *most effective* ways to sell high-ticket coaching, courses, or memberships. But most creators procrastinate because the structure feels overwhelming. You give them the exact words to say and slides to use—so they can confidently present and convert.

Perfect for:

- Coaches and digital product sellers
- Christian authors and course creators
- Affiliate marketers or high-ticket service providers
- Workshop leaders and summit hosts

Where to Sell or Offer It

- **Fiverr & Upwork**: "Webinar Script + Slide Copywriting"
- **Facebook Groups**: Coaches, course creators, and consultants
- **Instagram & LinkedIn**: Share snippets of your slides or script structures
- **Your Website**: Offer a full *Webinar Launch Kit*
- **Email List**: Lead with a free webinar title checklist to upsell script services

What You'll Need

- ChatGPT to generate webinar copy and scripts
- Canva or PowerPoint for slide templates
- Google Docs or Notion for script delivery
- Optional: Email automation experience if bundling reminders

How Much You Can Charge

- **Webinar Script Only (with CTA)**: $150–$300
- **Script + Slides (Full Presentation)**: $400–$750
- **Full Funnel Bundle (Script + Slides + Emails)**: $1,000+
- **Webinar Template Packs**: $39–$79 (DIY creators)

Just 5 clients at $500 = $2,500. 100 template sales at $49 = $4,900/month passive.

Tips to Stand Out

- Niche your kits: "Webinar for Christian Women in Business," "Faith-Driven Coaches," "Course Launch Masterclass Kits"
- Offer slide copy *and* visual design for extra value
- Bundle with **Email Sequences (#43)**, **Course Outlines (#64)**, or **Lead Magnet Funnels (#54)**
- Include a "How to Deliver Your Webinar with Confidence" guide or checklist

74. Sell AI-Generated Monthly Content Calendars for Niche Creators and Businesses

Every content creator wants to stay consistent—but planning content week after week is exhausting. With AI, you can create and sell **done-for-you monthly content calendars** that include daily post ideas, captions, and prompts tailored to specific niches—making it easy for creators to show up online every day with purpose.

What You'll Do

You'll use AI to generate:

- 30 days of post ideas or prompts (organized by day or theme)
- Optional captions or writing prompts for each idea
- Weekly or monthly content themes (e.g., "Testimony Tuesday," "Faith Friday")
- CTAs, hashtags, and engagement boosters
- Bonus: Reel/script ideas or seasonal promos

Example prompts:
"Create a 30-day Instagram content calendar for a Christian business coach. Include a mix of scripture-based motivation, business tips, personal stories, and product mentions."
"Write a July content calendar for an Etsy seller of digital planners. Include promo posts, behind-the-scenes ideas, and holiday tie-ins."
Deliverables can include:

- Google Sheets or Notion boards
- Canva-designed printable calendars
- Trello templates with weekly task cards
- Monthly PDF content drop for subscribers

Why It Works

Content calendars are an *evergreen* need. Creators, coaches, ministries, and shop owners all struggle with what to post. You're helping them stay visible, serve their audience, and build trust—without burnout.
Perfect for:

- Faith-based coaches and creators
- Etsy or Shopify sellers
- Service providers and freelancers

- Ministry leaders or speakers
- Social media managers

Where to Sell or Offer It

- **Etsy & Gumroad**: Sell downloadable calendars and planners
- **Fiverr**: Offer monthly content planning services
- **Facebook Groups**: Post sample calendars in creator or entrepreneur groups
- **Instagram or TikTok**: Show "What to post this week" Reels with a link to your kit
- **Your Website**: Launch a monthly subscription service

What You'll Need

- ChatGPT to write prompts, captions, and theme ideas
- Google Docs, Sheets, or Canva for formatting
- Optional: Trello or Notion if offering editable board templates
- Optional: Email automation if offering as a subscription

How Much You Can Charge

- **Single Month Content Calendar (PDF)**: $15–$29
- **3-Month Seasonal Bundle**: $49–$89
- **Branded Custom Content Calendar**: $150–$300/month
- **Subscription Plan (Monthly Content Drop)**: $19–$39/month recurring

Sell 100 calendars at $29 = $2,900. Get 50 subscribers at $25/month = $1,250 in recurring income.

Tips to Stand Out

- Offer niche calendars: "Faith-Based Women Creators," "Digital Product Shops," "Coaches and Course Creators," "Youth Pastors"
- Include holidays, scripture of the day, or quote prompts
- Bundle with **Caption Packs (#45)**, **Quote Packs (#69)**, or **Reel Scripts (#46)**
- Add a "Plug & Post" upgrade with done-for-you graphics

75. Use AI to Create Lead Magnet Mini-eBooks and Free Resource Guides

Email lists are still the foundation of online business—and lead magnets are the bait. With AI, you can create and sell **ready-to-use mini-eBooks** and **free resource guides** that help entrepreneurs grow their lists and build trust fast. You can even offer these as a service, product bundle, or part of a digital funnel.

What You'll Do

You'll use AI to:

- Write 5–15 page mini-eBooks, guides, or workbooks
- Generate topic-specific outlines and quick-win content
- Add CTA blurbs that lead to paid products or services
- Suggest titles, subtitles, and promotional email copy
- Optional: Include prompts, scriptures, or devotional reflections (for faith-based audiences)

Example prompts:

"Create a 10-page lead magnet titled '5 Biblical Principles for Building Wealth' for a Christian financial coach. Include a short teaching and reflection questions."

"Write a free guide for Etsy sellers titled '10 Tools to Boost Your Printable Sales.' Include one-paragraph tips and links to free resources."

You'll package the content in:

- Canva mini-eBook templates
- Google Docs/PDFs for editing and delivery
- Funnel-ready opt-in page copy and email follow-ups (if bundled)

Why It Works

A great lead magnet builds *trust, credibility,* and your *email list*. Most creators struggle to finish theirs—or make one that truly converts. You're offering an easy solution: a professional, valuable freebie they can launch in 24–48 hours.

Perfect for:

- Coaches and consultants
- Digital product creators
- Christian authors and speakers

- Course sellers and content marketers
- Ministry leaders and nonprofits

Where to Sell or Offer It

- **Fiverr & Upwork**: "Lead Magnet Writing + Design Service"
- **Facebook Groups**: Promote to coaches, creators, and authors
- **Your Website**: Offer as a product or service
- **Instagram or TikTok**: Show off sample covers and lead magnet ideas
- **Email List**: Use a lead magnet about lead magnets to upsell the full service

What You'll Need

- ChatGPT for generating content and outlines
- Canva for cover and layout design
- Google Docs or PDF for delivery
- Optional: Email tools (ConvertKit, MailerLite) for building the funnel

How Much You Can Charge

- **Basic Lead Magnet Copy Only**: $100–$200
- **Copy + Canva Design**: $250–$500
- **Full Funnel Bundle (Opt-In Page + Emails)**: $600–$1,200
- **Template Pack (Editable eBook Formats)**: $39–$79

Sell 5 full-service clients/month at $500 = $2,500. Sell 100 template kits at $49 = $4,900 in passive income.

Tips to Stand Out

- Niche your magnets: "Faith-Based Business Owners," "Wellness Coaches," "Etsy Sellers," "Christian Authors"
- Include editable Canva + Google Doc versions
- Offer funnel setup or email sequence upsells
- Bundle with **Freebie Funnels (#54), Course Outlines (#64)**, or **Launch Kits (#58)**

76. Sell AI-Generated "Tripwire" Product Templates and Sales Copy for Low-Ticket Offers

Tripwires are low-cost, high-value offers that appear *right after* someone opts into a freebie—designed to convert leads into buyers fast. With AI, you can create **tripwire product templates**, **sales copy**, and **bonus bundles** that help digital sellers instantly monetize new subscribers.

What You'll Do

You'll use AI to:

- Create short-form digital products (e.g., checklists, mini-courses, swipe files)
- Write product descriptions and landing page copy
- Generate persuasive sales blurbs and CTA buttons
- Craft upsell/downsell copy to go with the tripwire funnel
- Optional: Write 3–5 bonus item ideas with quick content

Example prompts:

"Create a $7 tripwire offer for a Christian life coach helping women overcome fear. Include product idea, description, sales copy, and 3 bonus ideas."

"Write a sales page and email follow-up sequence for a $17 productivity planner tripwire. Target online business moms."

You'll deliver the content as:

- Google Docs or Canva mini-products
- Funnel copy packs (PDF or editable doc)
- Editable Trello boards for funnel layout and copy flow
- Plug-and-play bundles for digital creators

Why It Works

Tripwires turn *freebie signups* into *instant revenue*. They qualify serious leads and set the tone for future sales. Most sellers struggle to write copy that converts or create small but valuable offers. You'll save them time—and help them earn money on day one.

Perfect for:

- Etsy or Gumroad sellers
- Course creators and coaches

- Faith-based content creators
- Authors, speakers, and funnel builders

Where to Sell or Offer It

- **Fiverr & Upwork**: "Tripwire Funnel + Product Creation"
- **Facebook Groups**: Share tripwire success tips with lead magnet creators
- **Instagram & TikTok**: Show product-before-and-after breakdowns
- **Your Website**: Create a Tripwire Copy + Funnel Build Package
- **Email List**: Offer a free checklist "5 High-Converting Tripwire Ideas" to upsell service

What You'll Need

- ChatGPT to write product copy, blurbs, and bonus content
- Canva or Google Docs for creating tripwire products
- Optional: Email sequence and checkout tool (ConvertKit, ThriveCart, etc.)
- Grammarly or Hemingway to polish the copy

How Much You Can Charge

- **Tripwire Copy Only**: $100–$250
- **Product + Copy Bundle**: $300–$600
- **Full Funnel (Tripwire + Bonuses + Email Sequence)**: $750–$1,200
- **Template Pack (Tripwire Product Ideas + Swipe Copy)**: $39–$79

Sell 4 funnels/month at $500 = $2,000. Add 100 template sales at $49 = $4,900/month in passive income.

Tips to Stand Out

- Niche your tripwires: "Faith-Based Funnels," "Tripwire Kits for Etsy Sellers," "Course Creator Mini-Offers"
- Include bonus creation templates or email swipe files
- Bundle with **Lead Magnet Creation (#75)** or **Email Sequence Setup (#43)**
- Offer a "Tripwire in a Day" VIP service for fast turnaround

77. Create AI-Written Daily Affirmation Text Message Services (Faith-Based or Motivational)

Daily affirmations are powerful tools for mindset and spiritual alignment—but people want *personalized, consistent, and short* messages that uplift them without needing to scroll social media. With AI, you can create and automate a **daily text message affirmation service** tailored to different niches—faith, purpose, success, or healing.

What You'll Do

You'll use AI to write:

- 30–90 daily affirmations (faith-based, success mindset, emotional healing, etc.)
- Optional scripture pairings or reflective questions
- Short daily prayers or one-liner declarations
- Category-based affirmation tracks (confidence, clarity, purpose, etc.)
- A welcome message + sample text to introduce the subscriber

Example prompts:

"Create 30 short, encouraging text message affirmations for Christian entrepreneurs. Each one should be 1–2 sentences long and include either a scripture or success mindset phrase."

"Write 45 daily faith-based affirmations focused on healing from trauma. Include brief, empowering language that feels like it came from a supportive coach."

You can send the messages via:

- SMS tools like SlickText, SimpleTexting, Twilio, or Subtext
- Email-to-text automation (for basic setups)
- App notifications if integrated with a mobile experience

Why It Works

People love short, encouraging messages—especially when they're faith-filled or personalized. A daily text creates emotional connection, spiritual encouragement, and brand loyalty. It also positions *you* as a daily presence in your subscribers' lives, making it easy to upsell books, coaching, or products.

Perfect for:

- Christian influencers and coaches
- Mental wellness and mindset creators
- Authors and personal development leaders
- Ministries or accountability groups

Where to Sell or Promote It

- **Instagram & TikTok**: Show "Affirmation of the Day" samples with opt-in link
- **Your Website**: Set up a subscription funnel or free trial
- **Facebook Groups**: Especially in faith-based, wellness, or women's circles
- **Gumroad**: Offer pre-written affirmation packs for other creators to license
- **Email List**: Upsell text access as a premium bonus

What You'll Need

- ChatGPT to write all affirmations and message sequences
- SMS service provider for delivery
- Google Sheets or Notion to organize tracks
- Optional: Payment processor or subscriber platform (Stripe, Gumroad, ConvertKit)

How Much You Can Charge

- **Daily Text Subscription**: $7–$19/month
- **90-Day Text Access (one-time)**: $29–$49
- **Pre-Written Affirmation Packs (for other creators)**: $39–$79
- **Custom Affirmation Track (for coaches/brands)**: $150–$500

50 subscribers at $15/month = $750 monthly recurring. Sell 100 affirmation packs at $49 = $4,900.

Tips to Stand Out

- Offer niche-specific tracks: "Faith & Focus," "Kingdom CEO Mindset," "Overcoming Fear," "Healing After Heartbreak"
- Include 1–2 "voice note" bonus audio affirmations for upsells
- Bundle with **Devotionals (#66)**, **Quote Packs (#69)**, or **Journals (#37)**
- Create a 7-day free trial to build your list before conversion

78. Sell AI-Written Journal Prompts and Reflection Page Templates for Coaches and Creators

Journaling is one of the most powerful tools for transformation—but many people don't know what to write. With AI, you can create **guided journal prompts** and **beautiful reflection pages** that help coaches, course creators, and ministries provide deeper impact to their clients, students, or audiences.

What You'll Do

You'll use AI to generate:

- Themed journal prompts (gratitude, healing, success, relationships, purpose, etc.)
- Weekly or monthly reflection questions
- Scriptures, affirmations, or quotes paired with each prompt
- Bonus: Morning and evening check-in templates
- Layout suggestions for printable or digital journaling formats

Example prompts:

"Write 30 journal prompts for Christian women seeking clarity in their calling. Include scriptures and reflective questions."

"Create a 4-week guided journal experience for productivity-focused entrepreneurs. Each week should include a theme, 5 prompts, and a weekly reflection."

You'll package and deliver:

- Google Docs or Canva-designed journal pages
- Notion or Trello boards (for digital journaling)
- Printable PDF journals or inserts
- Plug-and-play templates for other creators to customize

Why It Works

Journaling boosts clarity, emotional health, and personal growth. Whether people are on a healing journey, growing a business, or deepening their faith, guided prompts *remove the guesswork*. You're delivering value that helps people think deeper and grow faster.

Perfect for:

- Life and mindset coaches
- Christian ministries and faith-based communities

- Course creators and digital product sellers
- Therapists, counselors, or self-help brands

Where to Sell or Promote It

- **Etsy & Gumroad**: Sell printable or digital journal packs
- **Fiverr**: Offer "Custom Journal Prompt Writing"
- **Instagram or TikTok**: Share journal prompts in reels or carousels
- **Facebook Groups**: Coaches, self-help leaders, and Christian creators
- **Your Website**: Offer guided journals as a lead magnet or low-ticket product

What You'll Need

- ChatGPT to generate high-quality journal prompts and affirmations
- Canva or Notion for layout and design
- Google Docs or Trello for organizing bundles
- Optional: PDF conversion for printable shop listings

How Much You Can Charge

- **30-Day Prompt Pack (Text Only)**: $19–$39
- **Full Guided Journal (with design + themes)**: $49–$99
- **Custom Coaching Journal Prompts**: $150–$400
- **Monthly Prompt Subscription (for coaches)**: $25–$49/month

Sell 100 prompt packs at $39 = $3,900. Get 25 subscribers at $29/month = $725 recurring.

Tips to Stand Out

- Niche your journals: "Faith Over Fear," "Healing from Heartbreak," "Purpose Discovery," "Vision Casting"
- Offer printable and digital-friendly formats
- Bundle with **Affirmation Packs (#77)**, **Devotionals (#66)**, or **Content Calendars (#74)**
- Add licensing options for coaches to use in their programs

79. Use AI to Create Interactive Workbook Questions and Lesson Recaps for Online Courses

Courses and group programs are everywhere—but most lack engagement tools that help students *reflect, apply,* and *retain* what they've learned. With AI, you can create **workbook-style questions, recaps, and lesson prompts** that course creators can add to their videos, lessons, or downloadable content to boost learning and completion rates.

What You'll Do

You'll use AI to:

- Summarize key lessons or video content into reflection points
- Write 3–7 questions per module that encourage deep thinking and personal application
- Create fill-in-the-blank, open-ended, and multiple-choice style questions
- Build weekly summary pages or checklists for action steps
- Include spiritual, emotional, or mindset questions (for faith-based or personal growth courses)

Example prompts:

"Write 5 post-lesson reflection questions for a module on overcoming self-doubt in a Christian women's course. Include 1 scripture-based prompt."

"Summarize the key points of a video lesson on time blocking and generate a 1-page workbook with review questions and a weekly action plan."

You'll deliver your work as:

- Google Docs or PDFs (printable or fillable)
- Canva-designed workbooks
- Notion or Trello lesson templates
- Slide decks for on-screen prompts during video courses

Why It Works

People don't finish courses just because they bought them—they finish because they feel *guided and connected.* Your workbook questions and

recap tools help creators turn information into transformation—making their course more valuable and results-driven.
Perfect for:

- Course creators and digital educators
- Coaches running group programs
- Christian teachers and faith-based mentors
- Authors offering book-based workshops
- Homeschoolers and ministry groups

Where to Sell or Offer It

- **Fiverr & Upwork**: "Course Workbook Questions + Lesson Recaps"
- **Facebook Groups**: Digital educators, Kajabi users, and coaches
- **Etsy & Gumroad**: Sell workbook templates and question packs
- **Instagram or LinkedIn**: Share side-by-side lesson-to-workbook samples
- **Your Website**: Offer custom workbook creation services

What You'll Need

- ChatGPT to summarize lessons and generate workbook prompts
- Canva or Google Docs for formatting
- Optional: Knowledge of course platforms (Kajabi, Teachable, etc.)
- Grammarly for polishing and voice alignment

How Much You Can Charge

- **Module Recap + Questions (per lesson)**: $50–$100
- **Full Course Workbook (5–10 modules)**: $300–$800
- **Template Pack (Editable Question Sheets)**: $29–$59
- **Monthly Workbook Subscription for Coaches**: $39–$89/month

Sell 5 full course workbooks/month at $400 = $2,000. 100 template sales at $39 = $3,900/month.

Tips to Stand Out

- Niche into formats: "Faith-Based Course Workbooks," "Wellness Program Reflection Sheets," "Digital Product Creator Tools"
- Include end-of-module prayers, declarations, or scripture memorization tools
- Bundle with **Course Outline Writing (#64)**, **Launch Copy (#58)**, or **Email Sequences (#43)**
- Offer licensing for coaching programs or masterminds

80. Sell AI-Generated Affiliate Email Sequences to Promote Other People's Products

Affiliate marketing is one of the easiest ways to generate income—but most people don't make sales because they don't follow up effectively. With AI, you can create **ready-to-send email sequences** that promote affiliate products in a personal, value-driven way—without sounding like a sales pitch.

What You'll Do

You'll use AI to write:

- 3–7 email affiliate sequences per product or niche
- Problem-solution storytelling to lead into the offer
- Educational angles, objections, and personal testimonies (real or suggested)
- Click-worthy subject lines and call-to-action lines
- Optional: "Waitlist," "Early Access," and "Last Chance" versions

Example prompts:

"Write a 5-email affiliate sequence for a Christian entrepreneur promoting a Canva template membership. Include storytelling and scripture-based encouragement."

"Create a 3-part email sequence for someone promoting a course on productivity for moms. Make it friendly, helpful, and include common pain points."

You'll deliver the content in:

- Google Docs or Notion
- Email-ready copy format with subject lines and CTA links
- Optional: Canva-designed email swipe cards or PDFs

Why It Works

Affiliate marketing works best with *follow-up*. A freebie opt-in and one email isn't enough—most buyers need a few reminders, stories, or value points before purchasing. You give affiliate marketers what they need: an easy-to-implement, plug-and-play path to sales.

Perfect for:

- Bloggers and email list builders

- Faith-based influencers and content creators
- Coaches or educators recommending tools
- Etsy sellers or Shopify users referring software/tools
- YouTubers and podcasters promoting affiliate links

Where to Sell or Offer It

- **Fiverr & Upwork**: "Affiliate Email Sequence Writing"
- **Facebook Groups**: Affiliate marketing, digital product sellers, course creators
- **Your Website**: Offer as a done-for-you copywriting service or swipe file
- **Email List**: Use a free "Affiliate Email Template" to upsell full sequences
- **Gumroad or Etsy**: Sell niche-specific email packs

What You'll Need

- ChatGPT for writing personalized, engaging emails
- Google Docs for easy formatting and delivery
- Optional: Email marketing tool access if installing for clients (ConvertKit, MailerLite)
- Optional: Canva if creating visual swipe files

How Much You Can Charge

- **3-Email Sequence**: $75–$150
- **5–7 Email Affiliate Funnel**: $200–$400
- **Affiliate Promo Copy Bundle (Emails + Social + CTA)**: $500–$750
- **Template Pack (Editable Swipe Files)**: $29–$59

Sell 5 copy bundles at $400 = $2,000. 100 template sales at $39 = $3,900 in passive income.

Tips to Stand Out

- Focus on specific niches: "Affiliate Emails for Christian Creators," "AI Tools Promo Kits," "Coaches Promoting Courses"
- Include a bonus affiliate marketing tips sheet or email schedule
- Bundle with **Lead Magnet Creation (#75)** or **Freebie Funnel Setup (#54)**
- Offer an affiliate content calendar or mini-training on how to send the emails

81. Use AI to Write YouTube Video Scripts and Talking Points for Content Creators

Creating consistent, high-value YouTube content takes serious time—especially when it comes to writing hooks, organizing talking points, and crafting clear calls to action. With AI, you can offer **YouTube video scripts and outlines** that help creators film faster, speak with confidence, and grow their channel more effectively.

What You'll Do

You'll use AI to:

- Write full YouTube video scripts (intro, body, CTA, outro)
- Create bullet-point outlines for talking head or vlog-style videos
- Craft scroll-stopping video hooks and title ideas
- Add timestamps and suggested visuals or B-roll mentions
- Optional: Include description text and hashtag suggestions

Example prompts:

"Write a 5-minute YouTube video script for a Christian entrepreneur explaining 'How to Hear God in Business Decisions.' Include a strong hook and scripture reference."

"Create a talking point outline for a 10-minute video on 3 ways to sell digital products on Etsy. Include a CTA to download a free lead magnet."

You'll deliver the content in:

- Google Docs or Notion
- Slide decks (if requested)
- PDF filming checklist (optional)
- Trello boards (for content planners)

Why It Works

Creators often have the knowledge—but not the time or structure—to script their thoughts. You help them stay consistent, clear, and on-brand, while also boosting SEO and viewer engagement through intentional scripting.

Perfect for:

- YouTubers and vloggers

- Coaches creating free video content
- Ministry leaders and faith-based teachers
- Affiliate marketers and digital educators
- Podcasters who record in video format

Where to Sell or Offer It

- **Fiverr & Upwork**: "YouTube Video Script Writing"
- **Facebook Groups**: YouTube creators, coaches, and content creators
- **Instagram or YouTube Shorts**: Show quick script hacks and CTA examples
- **Your Website**: Offer a YouTube Scripting Service or Subscription
- **Gumroad or Etsy**: Sell script templates or monthly script packs

What You'll Need

- ChatGPT for writing scripts and titles
- Google Docs or Canva for formatting
- Optional: Basic SEO research tools (Ubersuggest, TubeBuddy)
- Optional: Thumbnail headline suggestions or pairing

How Much You Can Charge

- **Full Script (4–7 mins)**: $75–$150
- **Outline + Talking Points Only**: $40–$75
- **Script Pack (4–5 videos)**: $300–$500
- **Monthly Script Subscription**: $99–$199/month
- **Template Pack (Editable DIY)**: $29–$59

5 recurring clients at $150/month = $750/month. Sell 100 script packs at $39 = $3,900/month.

Tips to Stand Out

- Offer niche script packs: "Faith-Focused Channel Scripts," "Etsy Sellers on YouTube," "Affiliate Marketers Growing with Video"
- Include title, description, and thumbnail copy as a bundle
- Bundle with **Content Calendars (#74)**, **Lead Magnets (#75)**, or **Blog Repurposing (#71)**
- Add a "How to Read This Naturally on Camera" bonus tip sheet

82. Use AI to Write Brand Voice and Messaging Guides for Creators and Businesses

A consistent voice builds trust—but many entrepreneurs don't know how to define *how* they should sound online. With AI, you can craft **brand voice guides** that help content creators, coaches, ministries, and businesses stay aligned in everything they write—social media posts, emails, product pages, and more.

What You'll Do

You'll use AI to generate:

- Brand tone definitions (e.g. bold, warm, faith-filled, playful)
- Messaging pillars and recurring themes
- "Do say / Don't say" lists to guide content
- Sample bios, slogans, and signature phrases
- Writing style notes for social media, emails, and product copy

Example prompts:

"Create a brand voice and messaging guide for a Christian mindset coach. The tone should be encouraging, scriptural, and bold. Include themes like spiritual confidence, purpose, and daily faith."

"Write a messaging guide for a productivity expert helping creative entrepreneurs. The tone should be high-energy, witty, and practical."

You'll deliver the guide in:

- Google Docs or Canva templates
- PDF brand kits
- Editable Notion docs for teams
- Optional: Visual references (colors, fonts, example posts)

Why It Works

When multiple people write for a brand—or even one person over time—voice can drift. A voice guide brings alignment and clarity, helping every post, caption, and email sound like *you*. This is especially valuable for teams, growing brands, or content creators working with VAs or ghostwriters.

Perfect for:

- Coaches, course creators, and digital product sellers
- Christian ministries or nonprofits

- Agencies and freelancers building personal brands
- Etsy sellers or boutique eComm brands
- Authors building multi-channel platforms

Where to Sell or Offer It

- **Fiverr & Upwork**: "Brand Voice and Messaging Guide Creation"
- **Facebook Groups**: Coaches, authors, creative businesses
- **Your Website**: Offer as a premium one-time service or bundle
- **Email List**: Offer a free "Find Your Voice" template and upsell
- **Instagram/LinkedIn**: Share messaging tips and voice snapshots

What You'll Need

- ChatGPT to generate tone descriptions, messaging themes, and content examples
- Canva or Google Docs for formatting
- Optional: Use Loom to explain the guide if delivering it to teams
- Optional: Trello or Notion if delivering as a brand board

How Much You Can Charge

- **Basic Voice Guide (1-page)**: $100–$150
- **Full Brand Messaging Kit**: $300–$600
- **Team Voice and Tone Training Bundle**: $750–$1,200
- **Template Pack (Editable DIY)**: $29–$59

Sell 5 full guides at $500 = $2,500. Sell 100 DIY template kits at $39 = $3,900 passive.

Tips to Stand Out

- Niche your service: "Brand Voice for Christian Creators," "Faith-Focused Coaches," "Messaging Kits for Etsy Brands"
- Include bonus: sample social captions, email tone guidelines, or brand tagline ideas
- Bundle with **About Page Copy (#59)**, **Email Sequences (#43)**, or **Instagram Bio + CTA (#65)**
- Offer a free "Voice Finder Quiz" or worksheet to generate leads

83. Sell AI-Generated Show Notes + SEO Blog Transcripts for Podcasts and Video Content

Most podcasters and video creators skip show notes or blog repurposing—either due to time or lack of skill. With AI, you can create **SEO-optimized show notes** and **searchable blog-style transcripts** that help them get found on Google, increase engagement, and repurpose their content into long-form formats.

What You'll Do

You'll use AI to:

- Write podcast or YouTube episode summaries
- Pull out key takeaways and time-stamped sections
- Write SEO-friendly blog post versions of the content
- Generate meta descriptions and episode titles
- Optional: Create quotes or tweetable excerpts from the episode

Example prompts:

"Write podcast show notes for an episode on biblical business strategy. Include a summary, 5 key takeaways, and a call to subscribe."

"Turn a 12-minute YouTube video about overcoming procrastination into a 750-word SEO-optimized blog post. Include subheadings and a CTA for the lead magnet."

You'll deliver your work as:

- Google Docs (ready to copy/paste to podcast host or blog)
- Canva templates or PDFs (optional if branded)
- Notion or Trello cards (if working with ongoing clients)

Why It Works

Podcast and video creators leave *a lot* of SEO opportunity on the table. Most people just upload their content and move on. You help them multiply that content into searchable, skimmable, and sharable assets—giving it way more life and reach.

Perfect for:

- Christian podcasters and faith-based content creators
- Coaches and course creators with YouTube channels
- Digital marketers and educators
- Authors or speakers building authority

Where to Sell or Offer It

- **Fiverr & Upwork**: "Podcast Show Notes + SEO Blog Repurposing"
- **Facebook Groups**: Podcast networks, creator groups, YouTube growth communities
- **Instagram & LinkedIn**: Show snippets or side-by-side "video to blog" transformations
- **Your Website**: Offer it as part of a content expansion or SEO bundle
- **Email List**: Offer a free "Show Notes Checklist" to upsell your services

What You'll Need

- ChatGPT for summarizing, formatting, and optimizing content
- Otter.ai, Descript, or YouTube transcripts to extract raw text
- Google Docs or Canva for formatting and presentation
- Ubersuggest or Google Trends for SEO keyword support (optional)

How Much You Can Charge

- **Basic Show Notes (per episode)**: $50–$100
- **Show Notes + SEO Blog (per episode)**: $150–$250
- **Monthly Content Expansion (4–8 episodes)**: $500–$1,000
- **Template Pack (DIY Podcasters)**: $29–$59

Land 5 clients/month at $250 = $1,250. Sell 100 templates at $39 = $3,900/month passive.

Tips to Stand Out

- Include bonus quote cards or tweetable content for each episode
- Bundle with **Email Sequences (#43)**, **Webinar Scripts (#73)**, or **LinkedIn Carousels (#53)**
- Offer a "Launch to Scale" content repurposing package for new creators
- Add scripture tags or faith-based takeaways for Christian podcasters

84. Sell AI-Generated Community Discussion Prompts and Engagement Scripts for Facebook Groups, Courses, or Memberships

Online communities thrive when engagement is high—but many group owners struggle to post consistently or spark meaningful conversations. With AI, you can create **engagement prompt packs** and **weekly discussion scripts** that help admins foster connection, accountability, and retention inside their Facebook groups, course communities, or private memberships.

What You'll Do

You'll use AI to generate:

- Daily or weekly discussion questions
- Themed prompts (Motivation Monday, Testimony Tuesday, Q&A Wednesday)
- Short story-based or scripture-based icebreakers
- Weekly reflection questions or wins check-ins
- Bonus: Poll questions or challenge prompts

Example prompts:

"Write a month of daily engagement questions for a Christian women's coaching group. Include scripture tie-ins and transformation-focused questions."

"Create 12 weekly discussion starters for a digital product course. Include value-based prompts and community-building questions."

Deliverables can include:

- Google Docs or PDFs (printable or copy/paste)
- Canva-designed engagement calendars
- Notion boards for organizing weekly/monthly content
- Trello cards with scheduled posting plans

Why It Works

Community is everything—but it dies without interaction. You help group leaders spark conversations, boost retention, and create safe, valuable spaces without having to post on the fly. This is a *huge value-add* for memberships, group coaching, or free Facebook groups.

Perfect for:

- Coaches and digital mentors
- Christian communities or discipleship groups
- Course creators and educators
- Subscription or accountability programs
- Ministry leaders and Facebook group hosts

Where to Sell or Offer It

- **Fiverr & Upwork**: "Community Engagement Content for Coaches & Group Leaders"
- **Facebook Groups**: Especially those run by coaches or creators
- **Instagram or LinkedIn**: Share sample prompts or group insights
- **Your Website**: Offer "Monthly Engagement Packs" or VIP setup
- **Email List**: Use a freebie like "10 Questions to Spark Group Growth" to upsell your prompt packs

What You'll Need

- ChatGPT to write prompts, scripts, and engagement themes
- Canva or Google Docs for layout and branding
- Trello or Notion for content calendar delivery (optional)
- Optional: Tailwind or scheduling tools for Facebook automation tips

How Much You Can Charge

- **Weekly Prompt Pack (4–5 questions)**: $25–$49
- **Monthly Engagement Calendar**: $59–$99
- **Custom Community Strategy Kit (branded + structured)**: $300–$500
- **Template Pack (for VAs or coaches)**: $39–$79

Sell 100 packs at $39 = $3,900/month. 10 clients on monthly custom plans at $99 = $990/month recurring.

Tips to Stand Out

- Niche your packs: "Faith-Based Coaching Groups," "Digital Product Course Communities," "Healing & Recovery Ministries"
- Offer seasonal or launch-based packs (pre-course warm-up or mid-course momentum)
- Bundle with **Journal Prompts (#78)**, **Affirmation Texts (#77)**, or **Devotional Packs (#66)**
- Include tips on when and how to post for max engagement

85. Use AI to Create Book Launch Press Kits and Media Interview Prep Sheets

Authors and experts want media coverage—but they often feel unprepared when it comes to **pitching themselves** or presenting their story clearly. With AI, you can create **done-for-you press kits** and **media interview prep sheets** that help clients feel confident, sound professional, and stand out to podcast hosts, journalists, or event organizers.

What You'll Do

You'll use AI to write:

- Author or expert bios (short + long versions)
- Interview talking points and sample Q&A
- Book or product descriptions (with headline and hook)
- Press release templates or story pitches
- Media prep guides (key phrases, pivot questions, quote-worthy lines)

Example prompts:

"Create a media kit for a Christian author launching a book on overcoming anxiety through faith. Include their bio, 5 suggested interview questions, a book summary, and 3 key talking points."

"Write a podcast prep sheet for a coach being interviewed about digital entrepreneurship. Include how to introduce themselves, pivot to their offer, and share one personal story."

You'll deliver the content in:

- Google Docs or Notion (for easy editing)
- Canva-designed PDF media kits (print-ready)
- Trello cards or folders with swipe files
- Optional: Loom video walkthrough or coaching script

Why It Works

Visibility leads to credibility—and ultimately, sales. But most authors and creators are either too busy or too unsure of what to say. You help them show up confidently, land more interviews, and make every media moment count.

Perfect for:

- Authors (especially self-published)
- Coaches and experts launching digital products

- Speakers, ministers, and ministry leaders
- Podcast guests and summit presenters
- Personal brands building a platform

Where to Sell or Offer It

- **Fiverr & Upwork**: "Media Kit + Interview Prep for Authors and Experts"
- **Facebook Groups**: Authors, coaches, speaker bureaus, media training forums
- **Instagram or LinkedIn**: Share "before and after" media kit samples
- **Your Website**: Offer as part of a book/course launch service
- **Email List**: Offer a free "Interview Prep Checklist" and upsell the full kit

What You'll Need

- ChatGPT to write bios, press releases, and interview prep
- Canva for designing media kits and swipe cards
- Google Docs or Notion for easy collaboration
- Optional: Loom for walkthroughs or coaching add-ons

How Much You Can Charge

- **Basic Media Prep Sheet (Q&A + Talking Points)**: $100–$200
- **Full Press Kit (Bio + Q&A + Book Summary + Visuals)**: $300–$600
- **Launch Week Media Toolkit (Email Templates + Pitches)**: $750–$1,200
- **Template Pack (Editable Kit for DIY Authors)**: $39–$79

Sell 5 full kits/month at $500 = $2,500. 100 templates at $39 = $3,900 in passive income.

Tips to Stand Out

- Niche your service: "Media Kits for Christian Authors," "Press Kits for Coaches," "Speaker Prep Sheets for Podcast Guests"
- Include mock interview practice prompts or a printable confidence checklist
- Bundle with **Book Launch Funnels (#58)**, **Email Sequences (#43)**, or **Brand Voice Guides (#82)**
- Create a *Pitch Like a Pro* mini-course or workshop upsell

86. Sell AI-Generated Business Planning Templates and One-Page Strategy Docs

Entrepreneurs—especially solopreneurs and coaches—often have ideas but lack a **clear plan**. With AI, you can create and sell **plug-and-play business strategy templates** and **one-page planning docs** that help people clarify their offer, audience, goals, and next steps—without needing a full business plan.

What You'll Do

You'll use AI to generate:

- One-page business strategy sheets (offer, audience, channels, revenue goals)
- 90-day launch or growth plans
- Offer clarity worksheets ("What problem do you solve? Who's it for?")
- Monthly goal-setting templates with scripture or affirmation tie-ins
- Startup checklists or decision maps (what to do first, next, etc.)

Example prompts:

"Create a 1-page business plan for a Christian woman launching a life coaching service. Include offer description, audience, messaging pillars, and income goal."

"Write a digital business blueprint for someone launching an Etsy shop selling printable journals. Include product focus, platform strategy, and weekly tasks."

You'll deliver the content in:

- Google Docs or Canva-designed templates
- Editable Notion workspaces or Trello boards
- Printable PDFs (for Etsy or digital planners)
- Optional: Bonus video or guide explaining how to use each section

Why It Works

People want clarity—but they don't want to read 60-page business plan PDFs. One-page strategies and guided templates help them take fast, focused action. You become their go-to tool for turning vision into structure.

Perfect for:

- Coaches and consultants
- Christian entrepreneurs
- Etsy shop owners and course creators
- New business owners or digital starters
- Accountability groups or mastermind organizers

Where to Sell or Offer It

- **Etsy & Gumroad**: Sell printable planners and templates
- **Fiverr & Upwork**: "Custom One-Page Business Strategy Template"
- **Instagram or TikTok**: Share planning tips and "biz clarity in 60 seconds" clips
- **Facebook Groups**: Christian business, startup, or planner communities
- **Your Website**: Launch a "Clarity Toolkit" or Business Starter Pack

What You'll Need

- ChatGPT to generate content outlines, strategy docs, and prompts
- Canva, Notion, or Trello to build templates
- Google Docs or PDFs for delivery
- Optional: Bonus explainer videos or mini-trainings

How Much You Can Charge

- **Single-Page Strategy Doc**: $25–$49
- **Full Planning Toolkit (3–5 templates)**: $79–$149
- **Custom Branded Strategy Build**: $200–$500
- **Monthly Planning Subscription or Club**: $19–$39/month

Sell 100 templates at $39 = $3,900. 25 monthly subscribers at $29 = $725/month recurring.

Tips to Stand Out

- Niche your strategy packs: "Faith-Driven Coaching Clarity Kit," "Etsy Seller Starter Sheet," "One-Page Plan for Kingdom Entrepreneurs"
- Include faith-based reflection questions, affirmations, or scriptures
- Bundle with **Content Calendars (#74)**, **Lead Magnet Kits (#75)**, or **Journals (#78)**
- Offer licensing for business coaches to use with clients

87. Sell AI-Written FAQ Packs and Help Center Templates for Digital Products or Services

Whether it's a course, coaching program, Etsy product, or ministry membership—**customers always have questions**. With AI, you can create **FAQ bundles** and **Help Center templates** that reduce refund requests, boost buyer confidence, and save hours in customer service.

What You'll Do

You'll use AI to:

- Write FAQ entries tailored to specific offers (downloads, coaching, tech, delivery, etc.)
- Format answers in clear, encouraging, and on-brand tone
- Create email response templates for common issues
- Generate refund policy explanations, login help, and access instructions
- Optional: Include a branded Help Center homepage layout for websites

Example prompts:

"Create a 15-question FAQ for a Christian life coach offering a 12-week mentorship program. Include payment questions, spiritual guidance boundaries, and missed session policies."

"Write an Etsy seller FAQ for a printable product shop. Include download instructions, mobile use issues, and copyright questions."

You'll deliver the content in:

- Google Docs or PDF packs
- Canva-designed Help Center one-pagers
- Notion or Trello boards (especially for internal team use)
- Optional: Email scripts or swipe replies for support inboxes

Why It Works

Clear FAQs reduce confusion, prevent complaints, and build trust—especially for first-time customers. You're offering an *invisible but essential system* that protects your client's time, reputation, and sales funnel.

Perfect for:

- Coaches and course creators

- Etsy and Gumroad sellers
- Christian subscription or membership site owners
- Ministry-based digital offers or nonprofit services
- Any solo business owner without a full-time support team

Where to Sell or Offer It

- **Fiverr & Upwork**: "FAQ + Help Desk Copy for Your Course or Shop"
- **Facebook Groups**: Pitch to creators, coaches, and small business owners
- **Etsy or Gumroad**: Sell FAQ template kits for digital shops
- **Your Website**: Offer an FAQ + Policy Setup bundle
- **Email List**: Offer a free "10 Must-Have FAQ Prompts" cheat sheet to upsell

What You'll Need

- ChatGPT to generate FAQ responses and policy blurbs
- Google Docs or Canva for formatting
- Optional: Notion or Trello if offering full help desk systems
- Optional: Loom walkthrough or VA training guide add-on

How Much You Can Charge

- **Basic FAQ Pack (10–15 Questions)**: $75–$150
- **Full Help Center Setup (FAQs + Email Replies)**: $300–$600
- **Branded Template + Copy Bundle**: $500–$1,000
- **FAQ Template Packs for DIY Sellers**: $29–$59

Sell 100 template kits at $39 = $3,900. 5 full-service setups at $500 = $2,500/month.

Tips to Stand Out

- Niche your offers: "FAQs for Christian Coaches," "Help Center for Printables Shops," "Support Packs for Online Courses"
- Include a branded "Customer Service Script Kit" with email replies
- Bundle with **Refund Policy Writing (#68)**, **Product Launch Kits (#58)**, or **Email Sequences (#43)**
- Offer a one-time "Done-for-You Help Page Setup" service for WordPress, Kajabi, or Podia users

88. Use AI to Create Client Welcome Kits and Orientation Email Sequences

First impressions matter. With AI, you can design **client welcome kits** and **onboarding email sequences** that help new clients feel supported, confident, and clear from day one. These kits build trust, reduce confusion, and set the tone for a smooth, professional relationship.

What You'll Do

You'll use AI to:

- Write welcome emails and onboarding sequences (3–5 part flows)
- Create client guides with timelines, policies, expectations, and FAQs
- Include success tips, session prep info, or bonus resource links
- Add onboarding checklists and milestone trackers
- Optional: Design branded Canva welcome kits or Google Doc templates

Example prompts:

"Write a 5-part onboarding email series for a Christian business coach. Include a warm welcome, scheduling info, mindset tips, and encouragement."

"Create a client welcome kit for a graphic designer. Include communication guidelines, turnaround timelines, and a quick 'what to expect' section."

You'll deliver:

- Google Docs (editable versions)
- Canva-designed welcome kits or PDFs
- Email copy formatted for ConvertKit, MailerLite, or Kajabi
- Trello or Notion onboarding boards (for premium setup)

Why It Works

An organized onboarding system increases client satisfaction, reduces questions, and improves retention—especially in coaching or creative service businesses. You're turning their chaotic "Day One" into a guided, joyful experience.

Perfect for:

- Coaches and consultants
- Faith-based mentors or course instructors

- Service providers (VAs, designers, editors)
- Agencies or freelancers with multiple clients
- Group programs and masterminds

Where to Sell or Offer It

- **Fiverr & Upwork**: "Client Welcome Kits and Onboarding Sequences"
- **Facebook Groups**: Coaches, VAs, and freelancers
- **Your Website**: Offer as part of a "Client Experience Bundle"
- **Instagram or LinkedIn**: Share screenshots of before/after onboarding kits
- **Email List**: Lead magnet: "5 Things to Include in Your Welcome Kit" → upsell full service

What You'll Need

- ChatGPT to generate email flows, guides, and welcome copy
- Google Docs, Canva, or Notion for layout and organization
- Optional: ConvertKit or MailerLite if installing the email sequence
- Grammarly or Hemingway for tone and polish

How Much You Can Charge

- **Welcome Email Sequence (3–5 emails)**: $100–$250
- **Full Client Kit (Emails + Docs + Design)**: $300–$600
- **Premium Onboarding System (Trello + Email + Templates)**: $750–$1,200
- **DIY Template Pack (Editable Kit)**: $29–$59

Sell 5 client systems at $500 = $2,500/month. 100 template packs at $39 = $3,900/month passive.

Tips to Stand Out

- Offer niche versions: "Faith-Based Coaching Clients," "Design Studio Clients," "Podcast Guest Onboarding Kits"
- Bundle with **Offboarding Templates**, **Progress Trackers (#72)**, or **Testimonial Scripts (#62)**
- Include scripture-based welcome notes or encouragement sections for faith-driven brands
- Upsell quarterly client experience audits or refreshes

89. Sell AI-Written Case Study Templates and Customer Success Story Frameworks

Great testimonials are powerful—but a **well-structured case study** tells a story that sells. With AI, you can help business owners, coaches, course creators, and nonprofits transform client feedback into **high-converting case studies** and **branded success stories** they can proudly share.

What You'll Do

You'll use AI to generate:

- Case study outlines: Problem → Process → Result
- Interview-style questions to pull the best details from clients
- Long-form case study copy (1–2 pages)
- One-paragraph success summaries for landing pages
- Quote highlights or testimonial snippets for social proof

Example prompts:

"Write a case study for a Christian entrepreneur who helped a client grow from $1K to $10K/month using biblical business principles. Include the client's struggle, breakthrough, and how the program helped."

"Create a customer success story for a course that helped a mom launch her Etsy printable shop. Include before/after milestones and a quote about mindset shifts."

You'll deliver in:

- Google Docs (for editing)
- Canva-designed story pages or testimonial templates
- Optional: Notion dashboards for tracking client stories
- PDF portfolios with visuals + client photos (with permission)

Why It Works

Case studies are high-converting proof. They're *relatable, data-backed,* and *emotionally compelling.* They're perfect for sales pages, lead magnets, social proof, and media kits—yet many brands don't know how to write them well. That's where you come in.

Perfect for:

- Coaches and mentors

- Christian businesses and ministries
- Course creators, agencies, and consultants
- Nonprofits and service providers
- Digital product sellers with strong customer feedback

Where to Sell or Offer It

- **Fiverr & Upwork**: "Case Study Writing for Coaches and Digital Brands"
- **Facebook Groups**: Digital marketing, coaching, and branding circles
- **Your Website**: Offer as part of a proof-building bundle
- **Instagram or LinkedIn**: Share story snapshots and before/after results
- **Email List**: Free download: "Case Study Framework" → upsell done-for-you service

What You'll Need

- ChatGPT for generating story outlines, quotes, and write-ups
- Canva or Google Docs for design and layout
- Optional: Loom walkthroughs or interview support
- Optional: Google Form templates to collect success data

How Much You Can Charge

- **1-Page Case Study (Written Only)**: $150–$250
- **Full Case Study + Branded Design**: $300–$600
- **Portfolio Pack (3–5 Stories)**: $1,000+
- **Template Pack (Editable DIY Kit)**: $29–$59

Sell 5 branded case studies/month at $400 = $2,000. Sell 100 templates at $39 = $3,900/month.

Tips to Stand Out

- Niche your services: "Faith-Based Client Case Studies," "Course Creator Success Stories," "Mission Impact Reports for Ministries"
- Bundle with **Testimonial Copywriting (#62)**, **Email Sequences (#43)**, or **Sales Pages (#58)**
- Include client permission slips and media release forms
- Offer a monthly "Success Story Capture" service for memberships or coaches

90. Use AI to Write Objection-Handling Scripts and "Why This Offer" Sales Messages

Many buyers don't say **yes** because of unresolved objections—pricing, timing, self-doubt, or past experiences. With AI, you can create **objection-handling copy** and **"Why Now" messaging scripts** that help course creators, coaches, and digital product sellers overcome resistance *before* it stops the sale.

What You'll Do

You'll use AI to generate:

- Objection-handling scripts for sales calls, DMs, or webinars
- "Why this offer?" and "Why now?" email blurbs
- Social media captions that flip objections into confidence
- FAQs framed as subtle objection handling
- CTA language that reassures and builds urgency

Example prompts:

"Write a 5-point objection-handling script for a Christian coach selling a $497 program. Include answers to: 'I don't have time,' 'I've tried before,' and 'I'm not sure this will work for me.'"

"Create a series of Instagram captions that address common objections to buying a digital product—especially cost, tech fear, and overwhelm."

You'll deliver:

- Google Docs with categorized scripts (sales page, DMs, captions, webinar slides)
- Canva quote graphics or social templates (optional)
- Email sequence additions or plug-ins for launch funnels
- Optional: Audio script templates for reels or story voiceovers

Why It Works

Your clients already have great offers—but sales fall apart when objections go unspoken or unaddressed. These scripts close that gap, gently walking potential buyers through their resistance and into action—with empathy, confidence, and clarity.

Perfect for:

- Coaches, course creators, and membership owners
- Faith-based businesses with heart-led offers
- Etsy sellers or digital creators with mid- to high-ticket items
- Agencies and consultants in discovery call situations
- Launching products or relaunching existing offers

Where to Sell or Offer It

- **Fiverr & Upwork**: "Objection Handling Copy for Coaches or Launches"
- **Facebook Groups**: Post examples inside digital product or coaching circles
- **Instagram Reels or Stories**: Show "how to flip this objection" with your script tips
- **Your Website**: Offer it as part of a Sales Copy Booster bundle
- **Email List**: Freebie: "Top 7 Objections and How to Answer Them" → upsell full script package

What You'll Need

- ChatGPT to write each scenario
- Google Docs or Canva for formatting
- Optional: Email automation tool if plugging into follow-up flows
- Optional: Trello or Notion for organizing objections by product or persona

How Much You Can Charge

- **Script Pack (5–7 objections + responses)**: $150–$250
- **Full Objection Handling System (DMs, Email, Webinar)**: $400–$800
- **Sales Page Booster Add-On**: $250+
- **Template Pack (Editable)**: $29–$59

Sell 100 script kits at $39 = $3,900/month. Land 4 high-ticket clients at $500 = $2,000.

Tips to Stand Out

- Offer niche packs: "Objection Scripts for Christian Coaches," "Digital Product Resistance Busters," "Etsy Shop 'Why Buy Now' Captions"
- Include before/after comparisons to show impact
- Bundle with **Sales Page Copy (#58)**, **Launch Webinar Scripts (#73)**, or **DM Templates**
- Offer quarterly updates for recurring objection trends in your client's niche

91. Use AI to Create High-Converting Affiliate Program Toolkits for Coaches and Digital Product Sellers

Affiliate marketing is one of the **best growth strategies**, but most small business owners don't know how to set it up properly. With AI, you can create **plug-and-play affiliate toolkits** that give product creators everything they need to launch or boost an affiliate program—*without lifting a finger.*

What You'll Do

You'll use AI to write:

- Affiliate welcome emails and onboarding sequences
- Promo email templates affiliates can copy + paste
- Swipe files for social media captions, stories, and CTAs
- Product description blurbs and suggested hashtags
- FAQs, commission structures, and affiliate "do's and don'ts"

Example prompts:

"Create a full affiliate toolkit for a Christian author launching a $27 devotional. Include 3 promo emails, 5 IG captions, and a 1-page overview of the program."

"Write a welcome email and promo content pack for affiliates promoting a $197 digital course. Include positioning tips, audience alignment, and bonus CTA templates."

Deliverables include:

- Google Docs or Notion "Affiliate Vault"
- Canva-designed promo guides or branded swipe files
- Trello boards or ClickUp templates for affiliates to track content
- Optional: Affiliate scoreboards, bonuses, or leaderboard prompts

Why It Works

Affiliate partners are *free marketers*—but only when they're equipped. Most creators don't make time to write swipe files or support materials. You give them a complete package that turns *random referrals* into *intentional promoters.*

Perfect for:

- Coaches with courses or group programs
- Etsy/Gumroad sellers with referral bonuses
- Christian authors or ministries with product lines
- Digital product sellers scaling reach
- SaaS tool creators with influencer partners

Where to Sell or Offer It

- **Fiverr & Upwork**: "Affiliate Toolkit for Course Creators or Product Sellers"
- **Facebook Groups**: Pitch to coaches, authors, and sellers launching soon
- **Instagram/TikTok**: Share snippets like "What to Include in Your Affiliate Kit"
- **Your Website**: Offer as part of a "Product Launch Support Bundle"
- **Email List**: Free download: "5 Must-Have Affiliate Templates" → upsell the full kit

What You'll Need

- ChatGPT to write swipe copy, welcome emails, and FAQs
- Canva or Google Docs to organize promo packs
- Optional: Airtable/Trello setup if building a full affiliate dashboard
- Optional: Loom walkthrough for onboarding affiliates

How Much You Can Charge

- **Basic Affiliate Pack (Emails + Social)**: $150–$250
- **Full Affiliate Program Toolkit**: $400–$800
- **Affiliate Launch Bundle (for course/product launch)**: $1,000+
- **DIY Template Pack**: $39–$79

Sell 5 full affiliate kits/month at $500 = $2,500. Sell 100 template kits at $49 = $4,900/month.

Tips to Stand Out

- Niche your kits: "Affiliate Packs for Christian Creators," "Swipe Files for Etsy Promos," "Course Launch Affiliate Kits"
- Bundle with **Tripwire Funnels (#76)**, **Email Sequences (#43)**, or **Sales Pages (#58)**
- Include bonuses like affiliate tracking templates or leaderboard scripts
- Offer recurring kit updates to match product launches or seasons

92. Use AI to Write 365-Day Email Devotional or Motivational Series for Subscription Models

Daily emails are one of the *strongest tools* for building a relationship with an audience—but writing fresh content every single day? That's overwhelming. With AI, you can create **full-year devotional or motivational email sequences** that serve as high-value, faith-based or mindset-driven subscriptions.

What You'll Do

You'll use AI to generate:

- 365 daily devotionals, motivational insights, or short reflections
- Each with a scripture, affirmation, or mindset nugget
- Optional: A short prayer, journaling prompt, or action step
- Email subject lines and preview text for every day
- Monthly themes or spiritual growth focuses (optional)

Example prompts:

"Write a 365-day email devotional for Christian entrepreneurs. Each email should include a scripture, business principle, and short reflection."

"Create a daily motivational email series for moms who are building digital businesses. Include affirmations, encouragement, and simple focus challenges."

You'll deliver:

- Google Docs organized by month or theme
- Email-ready format for ConvertKit, Mailchimp, MailerLite, etc.
- Optional: Canva PDFs or printable calendars for cross-promotion
- Notion/Trello delivery calendar for implementation

Why It Works

Daily content keeps people *connected and growing*. Whether spiritual or mindset-based, this kind of sequence builds loyalty, reinforces identity, and sets up upsells into coaching, books, or group programs. Perfect for:

- Christian authors, influencers, or speakers
- Coaches with faith-based or motivational brands
- Ministries, nonprofits, or churches with email lists
- Course creators looking for high-value nurture flows
- Anyone with a message of encouragement or transformation

Where to Sell or Offer It

- **Your Website**: As a paid or free opt-in (with upsell)
- **Fiverr & Upwork**: "365 Email Devotional/Motivational Sequences"
- **Facebook Groups**: Christian entrepreneurs, authors, content creators
- **Etsy or Gumroad**: Sell themed packs (30, 90, 365 days)
- **Email List**: Offer a free 7-day sample to upsell the full experience

What You'll Need

- ChatGPT to generate daily messages with structure and voice
- Google Docs or email platform access for formatting
- Canva if offering printable versions
- Optional: Email automation knowledge for setup (ConvertKit, etc.)

How Much You Can Charge

- **30-Day Devotional Series**: $100–$200
- **90-Day Series**: $250–$400
- **365-Day Full-Year Series**: $800–$1,500
- **Digital Subscription (daily email access)**: $9–$19/month
- **Template Pack (DIY Creators)**: $49–$79

Sell 50 full-year devotional kits at $999 = $49,950. Add 100 subscribers at $15/month = $1,500/month recurring.

Tips to Stand Out

- Niche by theme: "Faith for Business Owners," "Emotional Healing," "Parenting with Purpose," "Building a Millionaire Mindset with God"
- Offer physical companion journals or planners
- Bundle with **Journals (#78)**, **Affirmation Texts (#77)**, or **Email Funnels (#54)**
- Add licensing for coaches or ministries to rebrand and reuse

93. Use AI to Create Accountability Message Templates for Coaches and Group Programs

Success doesn't come from information alone—it comes from **follow-up, encouragement, and accountability.** With AI, you can create **done-for-you accountability message packs** that coaches and group leaders can use via text, email, or app notifications to keep clients on track, engaged, and moving forward.

What You'll Do

You'll use AI to write:

- Daily or weekly accountability messages
- Progress check-ins, goal reminders, and mindset nudges
- Motivational boosts or scripture-based encouragement
- Short, punchy nudges for SMS, Voxer, Slack, or WhatsApp
- Bonus: Milestone celebration messages and "don't quit" pep talks

Example prompts:

"Write 30 daily text messages for a Christian weight loss coach to send to her group. Include a scripture, a challenge, and a word of encouragement."

"Create weekly accountability check-ins for a productivity coach running a 90-day bootcamp. Each message should ask about progress, encourage, and challenge."

You'll deliver:

- Google Docs or PDF packs by timeframe (30, 60, 90 days)
- SMS-formatted scripts (short, personal, easy to send)
- Optional: Canva quote card templates for visual motivation
- Notion or Trello cards for coaches to drag + drop into messaging systems

Why It Works

Coaching clients fall off without follow-up. These message kits help coaches **automate care**, **scale accountability**, and **boost retention**—without spending hours rewriting messages every week. It adds value *and saves time.*

Perfect for:

- Faith-based coaches (life, fitness, business, mindset)
- Group coaching programs or masterminds
- Challenge leaders or bootcamp hosts
- Course creators wanting to increase completion rates
- Church or ministry discipleship groups

Where to Sell or Offer It

- **Fiverr & Upwork**: "Accountability Message Packs for Coaches"
- **Facebook Groups**: Pitch to group leaders, challenge hosts, and Christian coaches
- **Instagram or TikTok**: Share sample messages or reels like "This text = $500 more retention"
- **Your Website**: Add to your coaching tools or group coaching starter kit
- **Email List**: Freebie like "7 Accountability Prompts" → upsell the full pack

What You'll Need

- ChatGPT to generate messages in different tones (tough love, grace-filled, excited)
- Google Docs or Trello for formatting and delivery
- Optional: Canva if bundling with visual quotes
- Optional: SMS tool integration support (SimpleTexting, Twilio, etc.)

How Much You Can Charge

- **30-Day SMS Script Pack**: $49–$99
- **90-Day Accountability Kit**: $149–$299
- **Full Group Coaching Toolkit (Messages + Progress Tracker)**: $400–$800
- **Template Pack (Editable)**: $29–$59

Sell 100 message kits at $49 = $4,900. 10 custom clients at $300 = $3,000/month.

Tips to Stand Out

- Brand your packs: "Faith-Based Accountability Messages," "Challenge Text Scripts," "Client Care Follow-Up Templates"
- Bundle with **Coaching Progress Trackers (#72)**, **Client Welcome Kits (#88)**, or **Devotional Texts (#77)**
- Add a "Message Delivery Strategy" tip sheet for best timing and tone
- Upsell white-label rights for other coaches to reuse

94. Use AI to Write Guided Challenge Series (3-Day, 5-Day, 7-Day, or 21-Day)

Challenges are one of the **most effective ways to engage, nurture, and convert an audience**—but most creators struggle to plan and write them. With AI, you can create **complete challenge series** that guide people day by day toward a breakthrough, habit, or result.

What You'll Do

You'll use AI to generate:

- Full challenge content (daily themes, teachings, and actions)
- Daily emails, texts, or video scripts
- Journal prompts, scriptures, affirmations, or checklist tasks
- CTA suggestions for each day (join the program, grab the product, book a call)
- Bonus: Pre-challenge welcome emails and post-challenge "next steps"

Example prompts:

"Write a 7-day challenge for Christian entrepreneurs on developing a faith-driven business mindset. Include daily scripture, teaching point, journaling prompt, and CTA."

"Create a 5-day digital declutter challenge for overwhelmed moms. Each day should include a short tip, reflection, and simple task."

You'll deliver:

- Google Docs with each day's content, email, and CTA
- Canva-designed workbooks or challenge sheets (optional)
- Email-ready sequences for MailerLite, ConvertKit, etc.
- Optional: Slide outlines or video scripts if hosting live

Why It Works

People love short wins. Challenges build **momentum**, **list growth**, **trust**, and a **clear path to your paid offer**. You give creators a done-for-you way to lead their audience into transformation *without the burnout*.

Perfect for:

- Coaches, mentors, and content creators
- Christian ministries and nonprofit leaders
- Authors launching books or study guides
- Course creators and membership site owners

- Etsy sellers launching faith-based planners or journals

Where to Sell or Offer It

- **Fiverr & Upwork**: "Custom Challenge Series Creation"
- **Facebook Groups**: Market to coaches, speakers, and group hosts
- **Instagram/TikTok**: Share challenge success stories or teaser content
- **Your Website**: Sell as part of a "Launch + Grow Toolkit"
- **Email List**: Freebie like "5 Challenge Ideas for Your Niche" → upsell your challenge packs

What You'll Need

- ChatGPT to write lessons, emails, prompts, and scripts
- Google Docs or Canva to structure and deliver
- Optional: Knowledge of email platforms (to plug in)
- Optional: Loom walkthrough or training on "how to run your challenge"

How Much You Can Charge

- **3–5 Day Challenge Script Pack**: $150–$300
- **7–Day Challenge + Emails + Workbooks**: $400–$700
- **Full 21–Day Challenge System (email + workbook + CTA strategy)**: $800–$1,500
- **Template Pack (Editable DIY Format)**: $39–$79

Sell 100 challenge templates at $49 = $4,900. Land 5 full-service clients at $700 = $3,500/month.

Tips to Stand Out

- Niche the content: "Faith-Based Challenges," "7 Days to Hear God Clearly," "5-Day Confidence Challenge for Christian Women," "21-Day Digital Product Creator Bootcamp"
- Add white-label licensing for coaches or churches to reuse
- Bundle with **Lead Magnet Funnels (#75)**, **Journals (#78)**, or **Text Message Sequences (#93)**
- Include a pre-built challenge launch calendar as a bonus

95. Use AI to Create "Start Here" Pages and Brand Intro Scripts for Websites and Funnels

People are landing on websites every day... but **don't know where to go** or what the brand is really about. With AI, you can craft **"Start Here" page content** and **intro scripts** that help creators and business owners guide their audience, explain their purpose, and lead visitors into action right away.

What You'll Do

You'll use AI to generate:

- Clear "Start Here" welcome messages (warm, guiding, and on-brand)
- Navigation sections ("If you're a ___, click here…")
- Personal intro scripts (written like a welcome conversation)
- Links to key offers, freebies, and next steps
- Optional: Video script or headline/copy for intro videos

Example prompts:

"Write a 'Start Here' page for a Christian author who helps women rebuild confidence after heartbreak. Include a short intro, 3 paths based on visitor type, and link CTAs."

"Create a personal welcome script for a coach's homepage video. Make it sound warm, confident, and purpose-driven."

You'll deliver:

- Google Docs (with formatted page copy)
- Canva wireframes or mockups for page layout (optional)
- Video script if the user wants to record a visual welcome
- Optional: Button/link copy for easy navigation

Why It Works

When people visit a brand site or funnel, they want **direction and connection.** A "Start Here" page builds trust, answers "what is this about?", and drives clicks to the *right* places—whether it's a lead magnet, podcast, product, or coaching program.

Perfect for:

- Authors and speakers
- Christian content creators

- Coaches, consultants, and mentors
- Course creators and community builders
- Nonprofits and ministry websites

Where to Sell or Offer It

- **Fiverr & Upwork**: "Start Here Page + Welcome Copywriting"
- **Facebook Groups**: Perfect for authors, creators, and personal brand sites
- **Instagram/LinkedIn**: Share examples of great vs. confusing homepage copy
- **Your Website**: Offer it as part of a "Conversion-Boosting Copy Bundle"
- **Email List**: Freebie: "5 Things Every Start Here Page Needs" → upsell full service

What You'll Need

- ChatGPT to generate brand-friendly, welcoming copy
- Google Docs or Canva for formatting or layout mockups
- Optional: Loom to guide users through how to add it to their site
- Optional: Headshot or brand visuals if offering full design support

How Much You Can Charge

- **Start Here Page Copy**: $150–$250
- **Copy + Video Script Bundle**: $300–$500
- **Homepage Welcome Flow (Start Here + About + CTA)**: $600–$1,200
- **Template Pack (Editable DIY)**: $29–$59

Sell 5 packages at $500 = $2,500. 100 template downloads at $39 = $3,900/month passive.

Tips to Stand Out

- Offer niche options: "Faith-Based Start Here Pages," "Speaker Welcome Scripts," "Coach Client Pathways"
- Bundle with **About Page Copy (#59), Lead Magnet Setup (#75)**, or **Email Welcome Sequences (#43)**
- Include tips for intro video recording and how to speak the script naturally
- Upsell a full "Website Words Bundle" for new brand launches

96. Use AI to Write Signature Story Scripts for Speakers, Coaches, and Entrepreneurs

Every powerful brand needs a **signature story**—a personal narrative that explains the *why behind the mission.* With AI, you can help clients craft an emotionally compelling, conversion-ready **signature story** they can use for speaking, websites, webinars, and sales pages.

What You'll Do

You'll use AI to write:

- 3–5 minute signature story scripts for personal brands
- Long-form "about me" stories with turning points and transformation
- 1-paragraph origin stories for bios, intros, and book covers
- Slide versions for keynotes or presentations
- Optional: Reels/short-form scripts for personal storytelling online

Example prompts:

"Write a 3-minute signature story for a Christian business coach who started out in corporate, hit burnout, and now helps women step into purpose."

"Create a transformation-focused personal story for an author who went from homelessness to published speaker. Include emotional beats, a faith angle, and a redemption arc."

You'll deliver:

- Google Docs with the full story and alt versions
- Optional: Video or podcast intro versions
- Story arc layout (Hero's Journey or Faith Journey format)
- Canva template for quote graphics or story highlights

Why It Works

People don't remember stats—they remember **stories**. A signature story helps build connection, credibility, and conversion. It gives creators the "why" they can share everywhere—from a sales call to a TEDx stage.

Perfect for:

- Coaches, authors, and speakers

- Christian influencers and testimony-based brands
- Course creators and personal development mentors
- Nonprofit leaders or brand founders
- Entrepreneurs building authority

Where to Sell or Offer It

- **Fiverr & Upwork**: "Signature Story Script Writing for Coaches and Speakers"
- **Facebook Groups**: Personal branding, faith-based business, author circles
- **Instagram/TikTok**: Share "story moments" or before/after scripts
- **Your Website**: Offer as part of a "Brand Foundation Package"
- **Email List**: Freebie: "The 5 Elements of a Signature Story" → upsell full service

What You'll Need

- ChatGPT to generate emotional, structured storytelling copy
- Google Docs for delivery
- Optional: Canva for quote cards or story visuals
- Optional: Loom walkthroughs or delivery with usage tips

How Much You Can Charge

- **3-Minute Story Script**: $200–$400
- **Full Story Pack (Long, Short, Intro Bio, Slide Format)**: $600–$1,200
- **Story-to-Speaking Kit (Story + Signature Talk Outline)**: $1,500+
- **Template Pack for DIY Storytelling**: $39–$79

Sell 5 story packs at $600 = $3,000. Sell 100 template kits at $49 = $4,900/month passive.

Tips to Stand Out

- Offer story angles: "Faith to Fortune," "From Struggle to Strategy," "Mess to Mission"
- Bundle with **About Pages (#59)**, **Book Bios (#85)**, or **Sales Pages (#58)**
- Add a "Share Your Story" social media script or audio version
- Include a workbook: "How to Practice & Deliver Your Story with Confidence"

97. Use AI to Write Short-Form Video Scripts (Reels, TikToks, YouTube Shorts)

Short-form video is *the king of reach* in 2024—but most people don't know what to say or how to say it fast. With AI, you can create **hook-driven video scripts** for Reels, TikToks, or YouTube Shorts that help your clients show up consistently, build authority, and get seen.

What You'll Do

You'll use AI to generate:

- 15–60 second video scripts
- Scroll-stopping hooks and 3-part content flows
- Calls to action for followers, downloads, or sales
- Faith-based, motivational, educational, or storytelling angles
- Optional: B-roll or scene change suggestions

Example prompts:
"Write 5 Instagram Reel scripts for a Christian money coach. Each should include a bold hook, biblical truth, and short takeaway."
"Create 10 short-form TikTok scripts for an Etsy shop owner sharing tips about selling printables. Include a question hook, one tip, and a CTA."
You'll deliver:

- Google Docs with scripts categorized by type (educational, story, FAQ, etc.)
- Optional: Canva templates for caption overlays or visual prompts
- Video storyboard versions (slide-by-slide or scene-by-scene)
- Swipe file of reusable hooks and transitions

Why It Works

Most creators *don't know how to start.* You give them structure, clarity, and consistency—so they can confidently press record and grow their platform. These videos become daily content that fuels their funnel.
Perfect for:

- Coaches and consultants
- Christian influencers or ministers
- Digital product creators and Etsy sellers
- Authors and thought leaders

- Membership or challenge hosts

Where to Sell or Offer It

- **Fiverr & Upwork**: "Reels & TikTok Script Writing"
- **Facebook Groups**: Creators, digital entrepreneurs, Christian business builders
- **Instagram/TikTok**: Showcase example Reels side-by-side with the script
- **Your Website**: Offer "Short-Form Video Vaults" or recurring script packs
- **Email List**: Freebie: "20 Hook Ideas for Viral Reels" → upsell full script kits

What You'll Need

- ChatGPT to generate concise, compelling scripts
- Google Docs for delivery and editing
- Optional: Canva or CapCut layout ideas
- Optional: Loom walkthrough or coaching add-on for delivery tips

How Much You Can Charge

- **10-Video Script Pack**: $100–$250
- **30-Day Video Content Pack**: $400–$700
- **Ongoing Monthly Script Service (30 scripts/mo)**: $750–$1,200
- **Template Pack (DIY Creators)**: $29–$59

Sell 100 packs at $39 = $3,900/month. Land 4 monthly clients at $500 = $2,000 recurring.

Tips to Stand Out

- Niche it: "Faith-Based Reels," "Business Tips for Course Creators," "Print-on-Demand Growth Reels"
- Bundle with **Content Calendars (#74)**, **Lead Magnets (#75)**, or **Repurposing Systems (#71)**
- Offer a "Record With Confidence" bonus: scripts + delivery tips + reels planner
- Create seasonal or launch-specific scripts (e.g., "7 Reels to Promote Your Black Friday Offer")

98. Use AI to Create "Evergreen Email Nurture Sequences" for Coaches, Authors, and Creators

Most people have *great offers*, but they lose connection with their audience between launches or product drops. With AI, you can write **evergreen nurture sequences**—a set-it-and-forget-it email series that educates, inspires, and builds trust over time.

What You'll Do

You'll use AI to write:

- 6–12-part evergreen nurture email sequences
- Story-driven content (faith journey, mindset shift, client story, lesson)
- Soft CTAs to products, podcasts, videos, or free gifts
- Plug-and-play onboarding + ongoing value emails
- Optional: Subject lines, preview text, and personalization tags

Example prompts:

"Create an evergreen 10-part email nurture series for a Christian author who helps women walk through healing after divorce. Include weekly encouragement, journaling prompts, and gentle product CTAs."

"Write an 8-part evergreen sequence for a digital product coach helping moms launch Etsy shops. Focus on mindset, strategy, and light promo."

You'll deliver:

- Google Docs (email-by-email format)
- Optional: Canva branded email layout templates
- Plug-in-ready version for ConvertKit, Mailchimp, or MailerLite
- Delivery map showing the flow of emails over time (PDF or Trello)

Why It Works

Most creators stop emailing after the welcome email. These evergreen sequences **keep their audience warm**, deepen the relationship, and softly lead to offers—**without having to launch over and over.**

Perfect for:

- Authors with digital products or books
- Coaches with signature programs
- Faith-based mentors and ministry leaders
- Etsy or course creators nurturing a freebie list
- Content creators building long-term trust

Where to Sell or Offer It

- **Fiverr & Upwork**: "Evergreen Email Sequence Writing"
- **Facebook Groups**: Especially creator, author, and coaching communities
- **Instagram/TikTok**: Show a sample sequence or flow diagram
- **Your Website**: Add to your "Email Funnels + Automation" package
- **Email List**: Offer a freebie like "My Top 5 Evergreen Email Topics" → upsell the full service

What You'll Need

- ChatGPT to generate story-based, voice-aligned email copy
- Google Docs or email software access
- Canva or Trello for visual flow (optional)
- Optional: Loom tutorial to show how to plug the sequence into automation

How Much You Can Charge

- **6-Email Evergreen Nurture Series**: $300–$500
- **10–12 Email Nurture Pack**: $600–$1,000
- **Full Evergreen Funnel (Opt-In + Nurture + Soft CTA)**: $1,200–$2,000
- **Template Pack (Editable DIY Emails)**: $39–$79

Sell 5 nurture packs at $600 = $3,000. 100 template packs at $49 = $4,900 in passive income.

Tips to Stand Out

- Niche it: "Faith-Based Email Nurture for Coaches," "Evergreen Emails for Digital Product Sellers," "Christian Ministry Email Series"
- Bundle with **Lead Magnet Kits (#75)**, **Affiliate Funnels (#91)**, or **Launch Sequences (#58)**
- Include a nurture strategy map + CTA schedule
- Offer quarterly updates or a "Done-For-You Evergreen Refresh"

99. Use AI to Create Faith-Based or Motivational Merch Slogans and Product Descriptions

From t-shirts and mugs to journals and hoodies—**merch with meaning sells.** With AI, you can generate **powerful slogans, scripture-inspired phrases**, and **product descriptions** for creators launching print-on-demand stores or motivational merch lines.

What You'll Do

You'll use AI to:

- Write original faith-based or mindset slogans (1–2 lines)
- Generate collections: "Confidence Collection," "Favor Over Fear," "Purpose Vibes Only"
- Add short descriptions for Etsy, Shopify, or Printful listings
- Create email or caption copy to promote the merch
- Bonus: Create quote packs or carousel posts to promote on socials

Example prompts:

"Write 10 bold, faith-inspired slogans for a Christian women's apparel line. Each one should be under 8 words and rooted in scripture or empowerment."

"Create product descriptions for a motivational mug collection with slogans like 'Stay Rooted' and 'Speak Life.' Make each one 2–3 sentences with a personal touch."

You'll deliver:

- Google Docs or Canva files with slogans + descriptions
- Optional: Printful product title + bullet list formats
- Social post or ad caption bundle
- Shopify or Etsy template if needed

Why It Works

Words have power—and when they're wearable or giftable, they spread fast. Creators often have the **vision and heart** but need help putting it into short, catchy, brandable language. You bring that to life.

Perfect for:

- Christian influencers or content creators
- Etsy or Shopify store owners

- Authors creating book-themed merch
- Motivational speakers and coaches
- Ministries expanding into merch for outreach/fundraising

Where to Sell or Offer It

- **Fiverr & Upwork**: "Merch Slogan + Product Copy Writing"
- **Facebook Groups**: Merch sellers, Christian entrepreneurs, print-on-demand communities
- **Instagram Reels/Posts**: Share "This slogan sold 200 shirts" breakdowns
- **Your Website**: Offer as part of a Merch Launch Kit or Branding Bundle
- **Email List**: Freebie: "25 AI-Generated Merch Slogan Ideas" → upsell full package

What You'll Need

- ChatGPT to create slogans, descriptions, and themes
- Canva for mockup ideas or carousel posts
- Google Docs for organized delivery
- Optional: Printful/Printify knowledge for easy export

How Much You Can Charge

- **10–20 Slogan Pack**: $50–$150
- **Full Product Launch (Slogans + Descriptions + Captions)**: $300–$600
- **Branded Merch Line Copy Bundle (5+ items)**: $800–$1,200
- **Template Pack (Editable DIY Format)**: $29–$59

Sell 5 full merch packs/month at $400 = $2,000. Sell 100 slogan kits at $39 = $3,900/month passive.

Tips to Stand Out

- Niche by mission: "Faith & Freedom Merch Copy," "Motivational Mindset Tees," "Scripture Wear Drops"
- Include scripture or affirmation variations per slogan
- Bundle with **Quote Packs (#69)**, **Instagram Captions (#45)**, or **Content Calendars (#74)**
- Offer white-label rights or sell slogan packs on Etsy

100. Use AI to Create Microcourse Outlines and Lesson Scripts for Digital Educators

Microcourses are short, actionable, and **perfect for fast results and passive income**. With AI, you can build **full course frameworks**, **lesson scripts**, and **launch content** that help creators go from idea to income *without ever opening a slide deck themselves.*

What You'll Do

You'll use AI to generate:

- Microcourse titles, subtitles, and transformation promises
- 3–7 lesson outlines (what to teach, in what order)
- Script or talking points for each lesson (video or written format)
- Slide bullets and worksheet prompts (optional)
- CTA ideas for upsells or next steps

Example prompts:

"Create a 5-lesson microcourse for a Christian entrepreneur teaching 'Faith-Based Goal Setting.' Include a title, brief outline, lesson scripts, and CTA ideas."

"Write a mini course framework for a digital planner seller teaching 'How to Start an Etsy Shop in 7 Days.' Include lesson titles and scripts."

You'll deliver:

- Google Docs with full course layout + copy
- Optional: Canva slides or worksheet templates
- Notion or Trello board to organize the course flow
- Email + social copy to promote the course (bonus upsell)

Why It Works

Microcourses are easier to create, easier to sell, and perfect for first-time digital product creators. You're helping people monetize their message—fast—and giving them content they can *launch this week.*

Perfect for:

- Coaches, consultants, and course creators
- Faith-based teachers and ministry educators
- Etsy sellers, service providers, and VAs

- Authors building companion courses
- Anyone wanting to package expertise into passive income

Where to Sell or Offer It

- **Fiverr & Upwork**: "Microcourse Creation + Script Writing"
- **Facebook Groups**: Coaches, authors, and digital product builders
- **Instagram/TikTok**: "I helped someone turn their story into a $37 course…" style content
- **Your Website**: Launch a "Mini Course Creation Kit" or service
- **Email List**: Freebie: "Microcourse Idea Generator" → upsell the full pack

What You'll Need

- ChatGPT to write course titles, lesson outlines, and scripts
- Google Docs or Canva to organize and deliver
- Optional: Trello/Notion to build the lesson flow
- Email automation tool for pre-sale or launch sequences

How Much You Can Charge

- **Microcourse Outline + Scripts (3–5 lessons)**: $300–$600
- **Full Course Pack (Outline, Scripts, Slides, CTAs)**: $800–$1,500
- **Launch Content Add-On (Emails + Posts)**: $300–$500
- **Template Pack (DIY Creators)**: $39–$79

Sell 5 course builds at $800 = $4,000/month. 100 template kits at $49 = $4,900/month passive.

Tips to Stand Out

- Niche it: "Faith-Based Microcourses," "Mini Courses for Coaches," "Passive Products for Etsy Sellers"
- Bundle with **Lead Magnet Funnels (#75)**, **Email Nurture Series (#98)**, or **Challenge Launch Kits (#94)**
- Include a "Monetize Your Microcourse" roadmap
- Offer licensing options or white-label templates for agencies

101. Use AI to Create and Sell Resellable Digital Products (Licensing-Ready Content)

One of the smartest ways to make money with AI is to create digital products that other people can **resell**. This means you're not just selling to customers—you're supplying other sellers. With AI, you can build products that come with **resell rights**, turning you into a content supplier in the digital marketplace.

What You'll Do

You'll use AI to:

- Create ebooks, templates, workbooks, or journals
- Write the content once, then package it with "resell rights"
- Include a simple licensing document (AI can write it for you!)
- Add promotional materials: product descriptions, email copy, and social posts
- Optional: Bundle multiple items together into a ready-to-sell business-in-a-box

Why It Works

Instead of making a single sale, you're creating a product that **others can sell too.** You become the source. This means you earn money upfront, and your buyers can use your AI-generated content to make money themselves—no extra effort from you after delivery.

Perfect resellable product types:

- Printable journals and planners
- Scripture-based devotionals
- Motivational or mindset ebooks
- Course workbooks and templates
- Digital affirmation decks or quote packs

Example

You create a 30-day gratitude journal with AI. Add a cover, license it for resell, and sell it for $49 to other creators, Etsy sellers, or coaches. They can now sell it in their shop, and you don't have to lift a finger after the sale.

Where to Sell It

- Your own website or Shopify store
- Etsy or Gumroad

- Inside Facebook groups for coaches, VAs, or Christian entrepreneurs
- Through your email list or Instagram page
- Bundle it with Canva templates for added value

Tools You'll Need

- **ChatGPT** to generate the written content
- **Canva** for covers and page design
- **Google Docs or PDF** for the product file
- Optional: AI-generated mockups for promotion
- A licensing doc (AI can draft this too—just ask!)

How Much You Can Charge

- **Single Resellable Product**: $29–$99
- **Full Resell Bundle (with templates and promos)**: $100–$300
- **"Business in a Box" Package**: $300–$500

Sell 100 resell licenses at $49 = $4,900. Bundle with 3–5 products for even more value.

Tips to Stand Out

- Add white-label options (buyers can rebrand the product as their own)
- Offer a simple explainer PDF so your buyer knows how to sell it
- Use AI to create bonuses like checklists, swipe files, or captions
- Make it niche-specific: "Christian Coaching Tools," "Self-Care for Moms," "Productivity Templates for Entrepreneurs"

Bonus Use AI to Create Educational Activity Books for Kids (Math, Reading & Bible Fun)

Instead of just storybooks, try using AI to create **educational activity books** for children. These books can teach **math, reading, handwriting, vocabulary, or even Bible-based learning**—and they're highly profitable on Etsy, Amazon KDP, or in homeschool markets.

What You'll Do

You'll use AI to:

- Generate word problems, reading passages, or learning games
- Create letter tracing or number practice sheets
- Write Bible-themed crossword puzzles or memory verse fill-ins
- Organize themed books (e.g., "Jesus and Numbers," "Faith & Phonics," "Bible Math for Beginners")
- Format pages using Canva or PowerPoint and export as PDFs

Example prompts:
"Create 25 math problems for ages 6–8 using animals from Noah's Ark as a theme. Include Bible verse connections."
"Generate 10 early reader paragraphs about kindness with comprehension questions and a coloring section."

Why It Works

Parents, homeschoolers, and Sunday school teachers are always looking for **faith-based and educational content** that entertains and teaches at the same time. These activity books are valuable, repeat-sellable, and easy to expand into a full series.

Where to Sell It

- Etsy (Faith-Based Kids Printables)
- Amazon KDP (Kindle Direct Publishing)
- Gumroad or your own Shopify store
- Church resource catalogs or Christian homeschool groups
- Bundle as a giveaway or upsell with children's devotionals

What You'll Need

- ChatGPT for educational content creation

- Canva or PowerPoint for workbook layout
- PDF export tool for printable file creation
- Optional: Clipart packs or DALL·E for themed illustrations

How Much You Can Charge

- **Single Workbook (20–30 pages)**: $7–$15
- **Bundle of 3–5 Books**: $25–$45
- **Custom Book for Churches/Schools**: $75–$150
- **Licensing Pack (for teachers or homeschoolers)**: $49–$99

Tips to Stand Out

- Focus on age-specific learning (Pre-K, 1st grade, etc.)
- Include prayer prompts or Bible verses in every section
- Brand it as a full curriculum series ("God's Little Learners: Volume 1")
- Offer black & white versions for easy printing

Made in the USA
Monee, IL
04 November 2026

67386633R00118